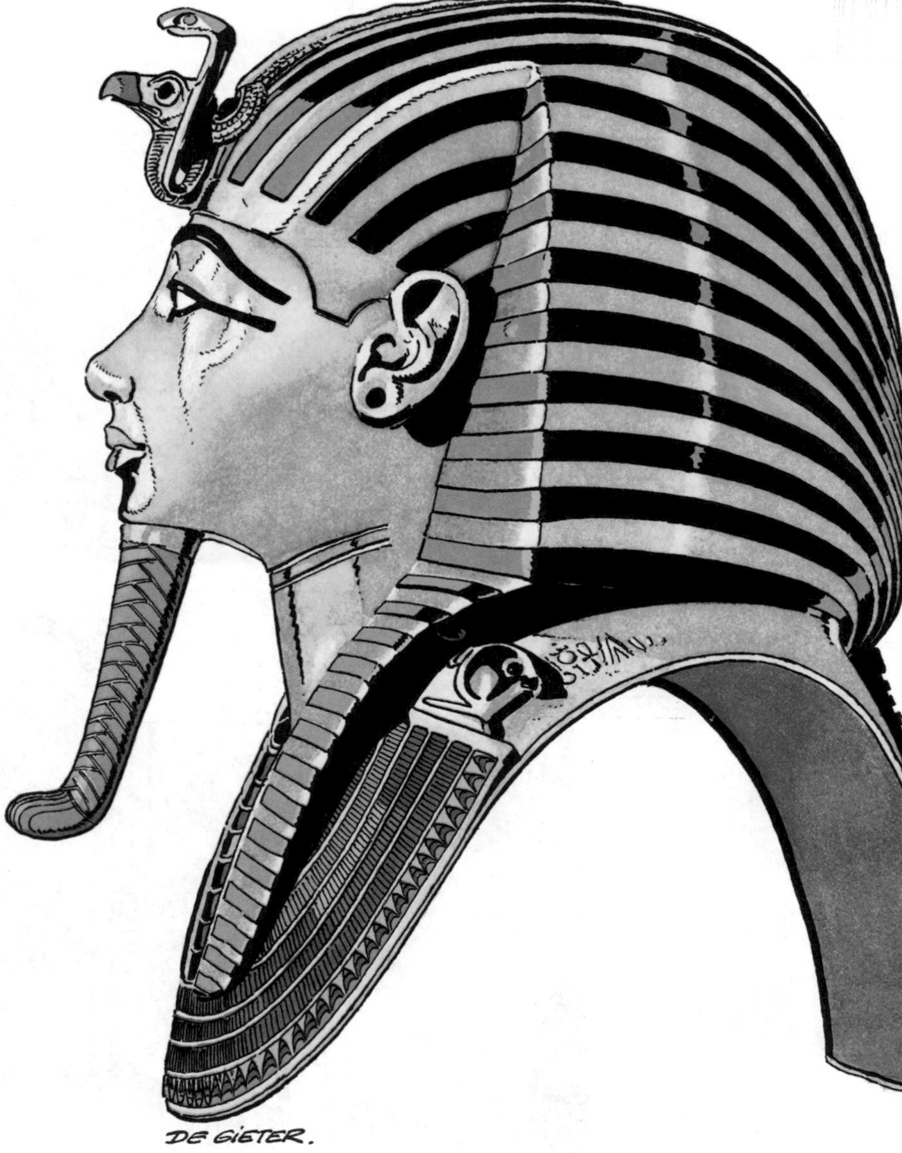
DE GIETER.

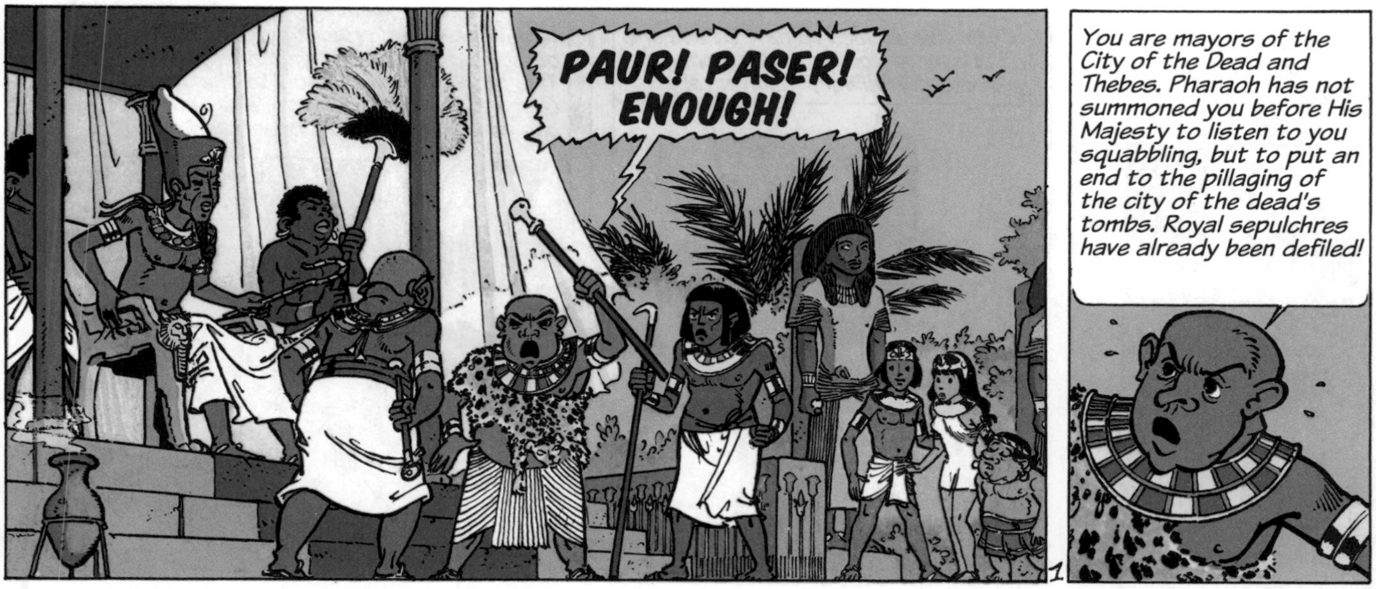
PAUR! PASER! ENOUGH!
You are mayors of the City of the Dead and Thebes. Pharaoh has not summoned you before His Majesty to listen to you squabbling, but to put an end to the pillaging of the city of the dead's tombs. Royal sepulchres have already been defiled!

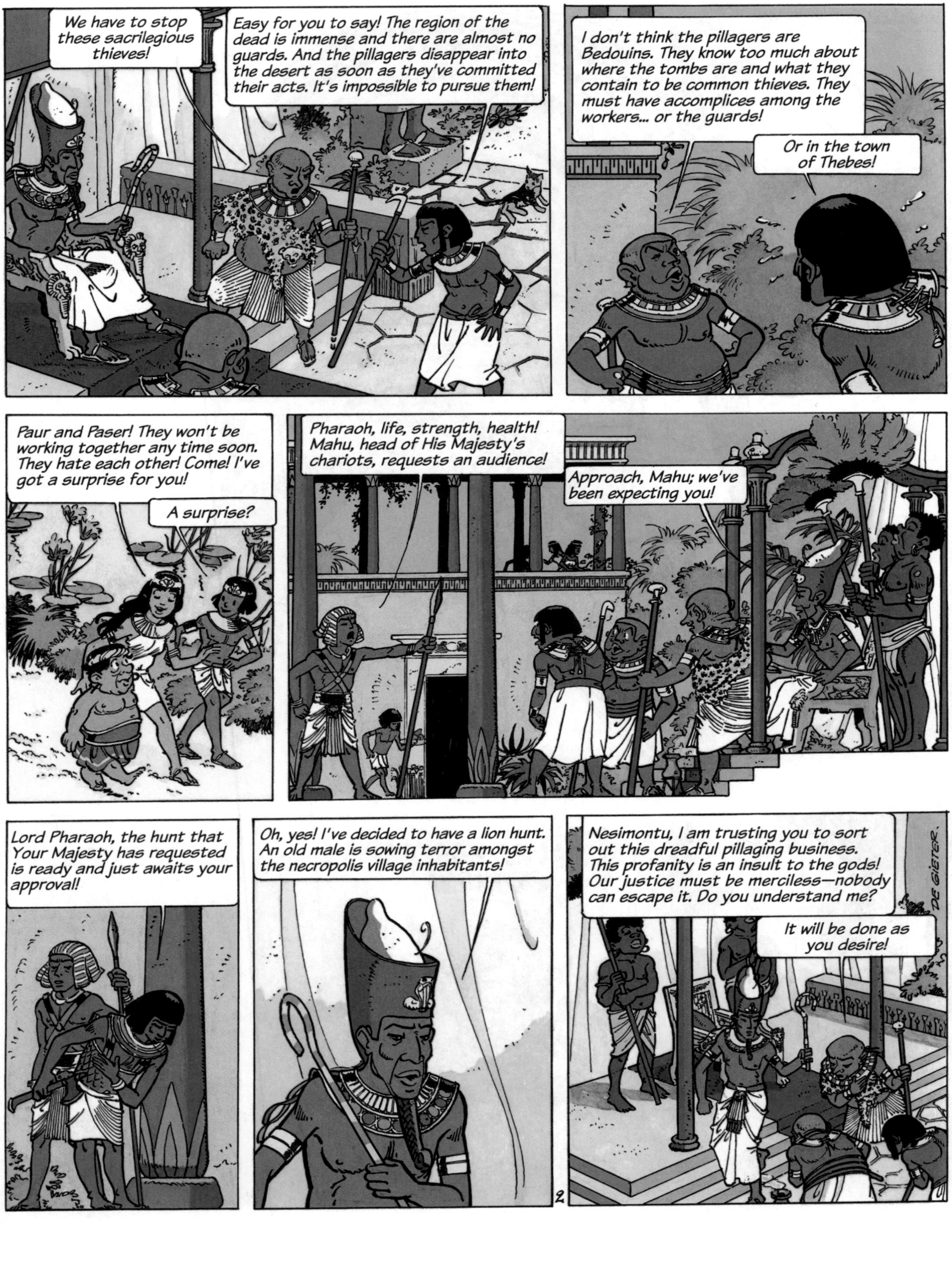
We have to stop these sacrilegious thieves!
Easy for you to say! The region of the dead is immense and there are almost no guards. And the pillagers disappear into the desert as soon as they've committed their acts. It's impossible to pursue them!
I don't think the pillagers are Bedouins. They know too much about where the tombs are and what they contain to be common thieves. They must have accomplices among the workers... or the guards!
Or in the town of Thebes!
Paur and Paser! They won't be working together any time soon. They hate each other! Come! I've got a surprise for you!
A surprise?
Pharaoh, life, strength, health! Mahu, head of His Majesty's chariots, requests an audience!
Approach, Mahu; we've been expecting you!
Lord Pharaoh, the hunt that Your Majesty has requested is ready and just awaits your approval!
Oh, yes! I've decided to have a lion hunt. An old male is sowing terror amongst the necropolis village inhabitants!
Nesimontu, I am trusting you to sort out this dreadful pillaging business. This profanity is an insult to the gods! Our justice must be merciless—nobody can escape it. Do you understand me?
It will be done as you desire!
DE GIETER
2

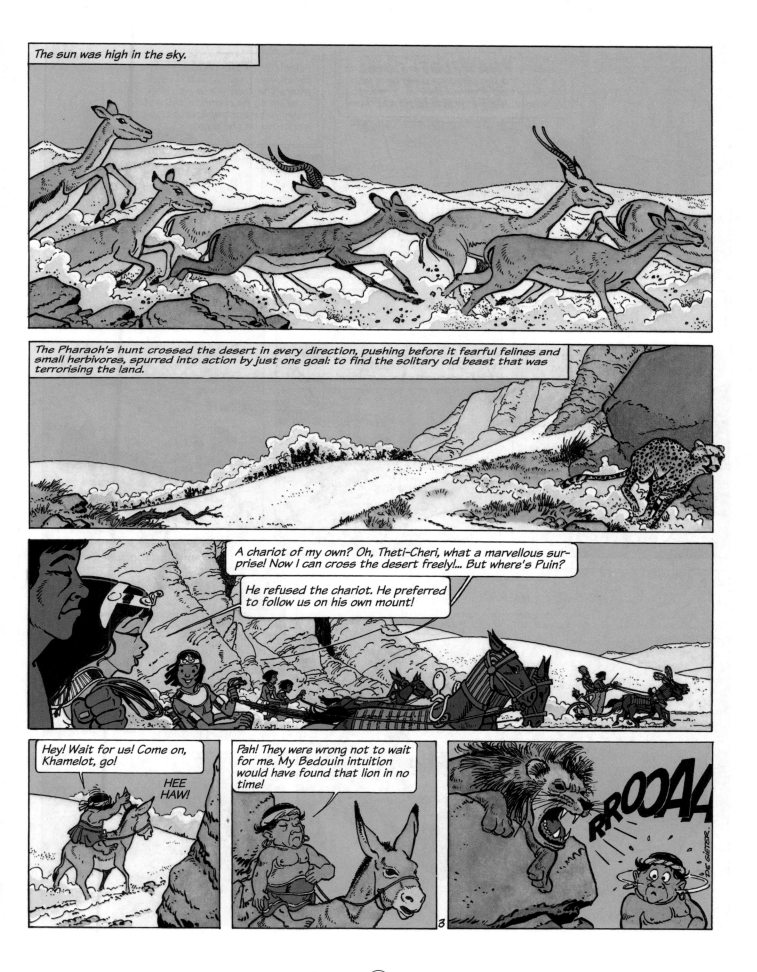

The sun was high in the sky.

The Pharaoh's hunt crossed the desert in every direction, pushing before it fearful felines and small herbivores, spurred into action by just one goal: to find the solitary old beast that was terrorising the land.

A chariot of my own? Oh, Theti-Cheri, what a marvellous surprise! Now I can cross the desert freely!... But where's Puin?

He refused the chariot. He preferred to follow us on his own mount!

Hey! Wait for us! Come on, Khamelot, go!

HEE HAW!

Pah! They were wrong not to wait for me. My Bedouin intuition would have found that lion in no time!

RROOAA

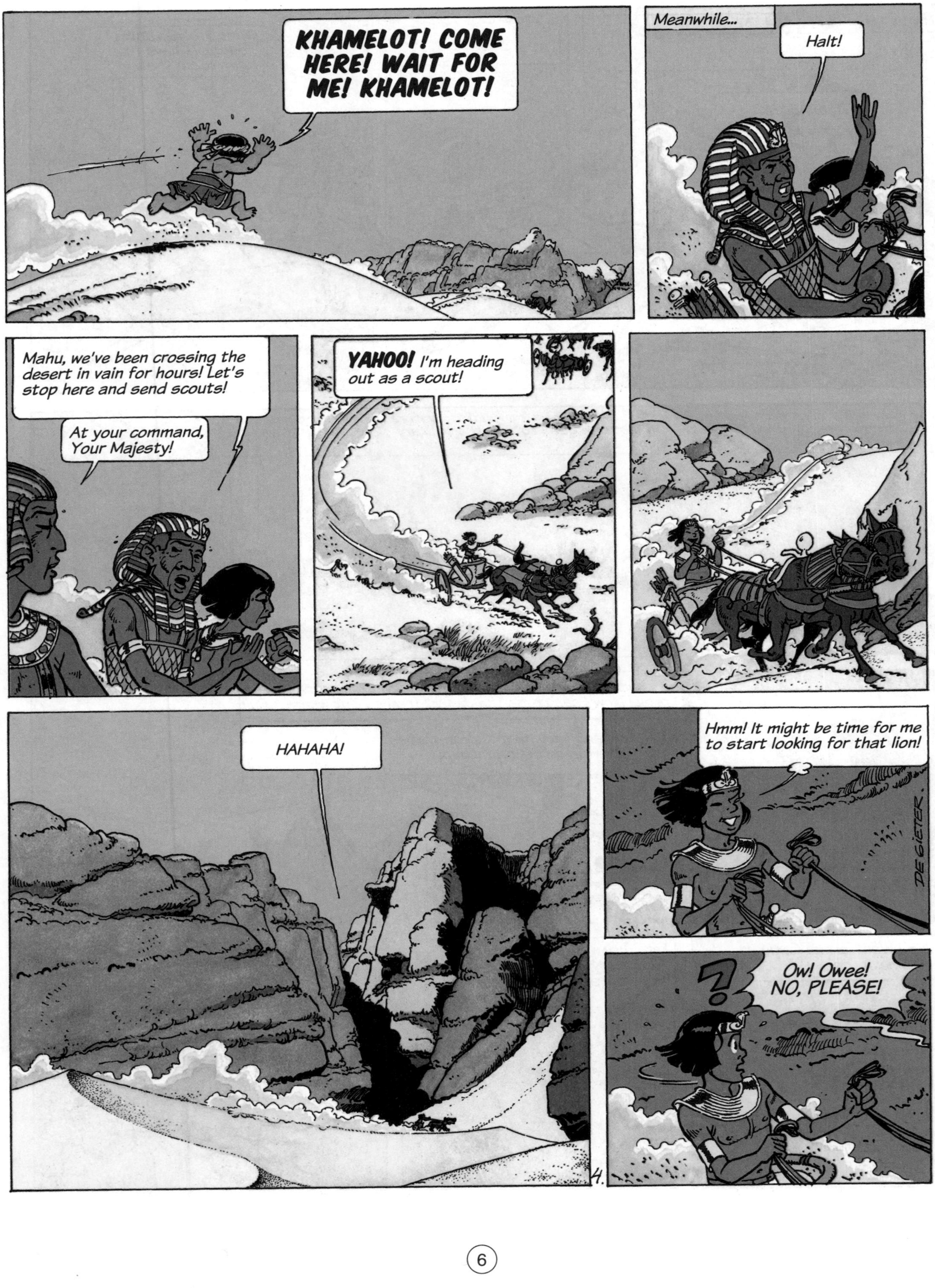

KHAMELOT! COME HERE! WAIT FOR ME! KHAMELOT!
Meanwhile...
Halt!
Mahu, we've been crossing the desert in vain for hours! Let's stop here and send scouts!
At your command, Your Majesty!
YAHOO! I'm heading out as a scout!
HAHAHA!
Hmm! It might be time for me to start looking for that lion!
DE GIETER
?
Ow! Owee! NO, PLEASE!

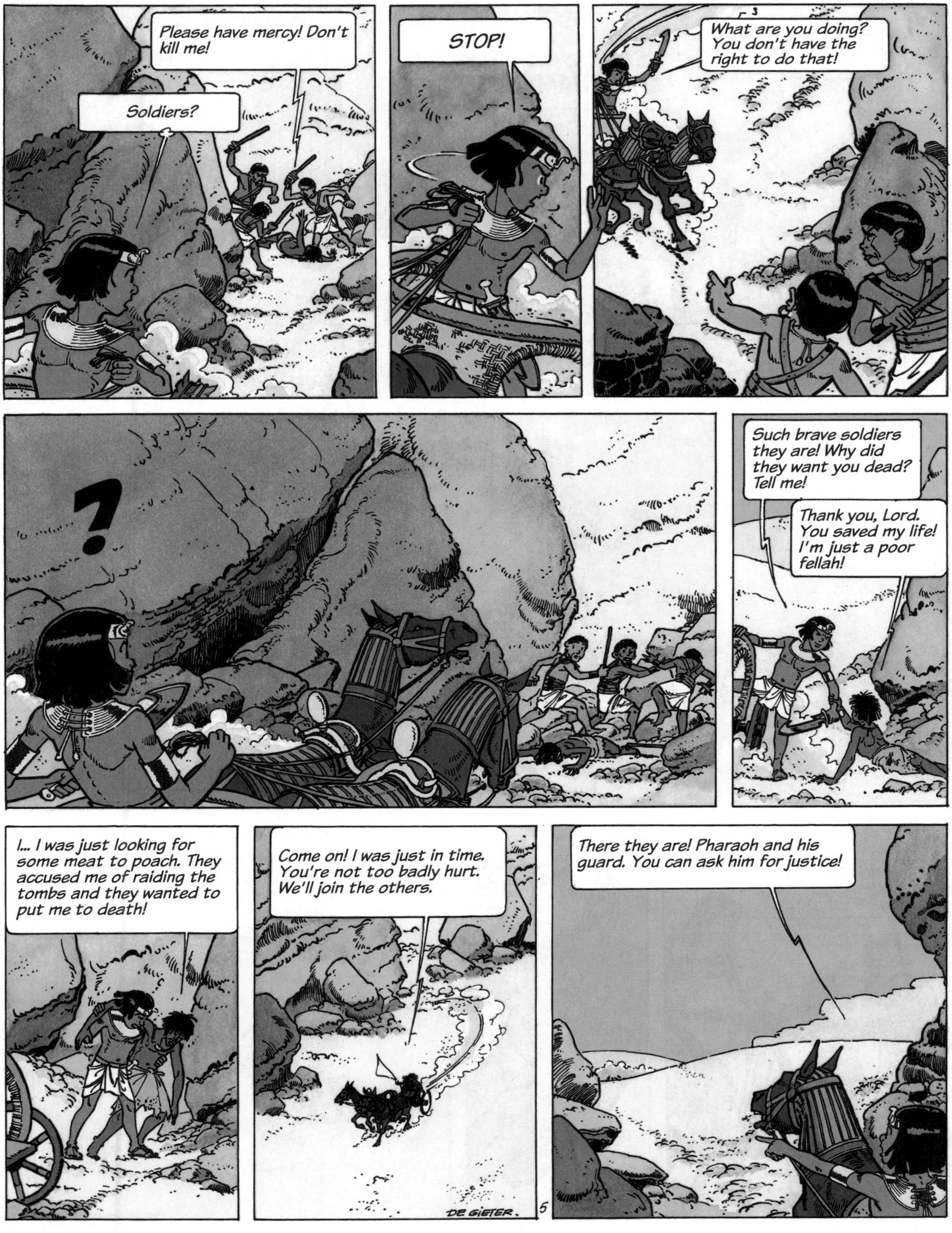
Please have mercy! Don't kill me!
Soldiers?
STOP!
What are you doing? You don't have the right to do that!
?
Such brave soldiers they are! Why did they want you dead? Tell me!
Thank you, Lord. You saved my life! I'm just a poor fellah!
I... I was just looking for some meat to poach. They accused me of raiding the tombs and they wanted to put me to death!
Come on! I was just in time. You're not too badly hurt. We'll join the others.
DE GIETER.
There they are! Pharaoh and his guard. You can ask him for justice!

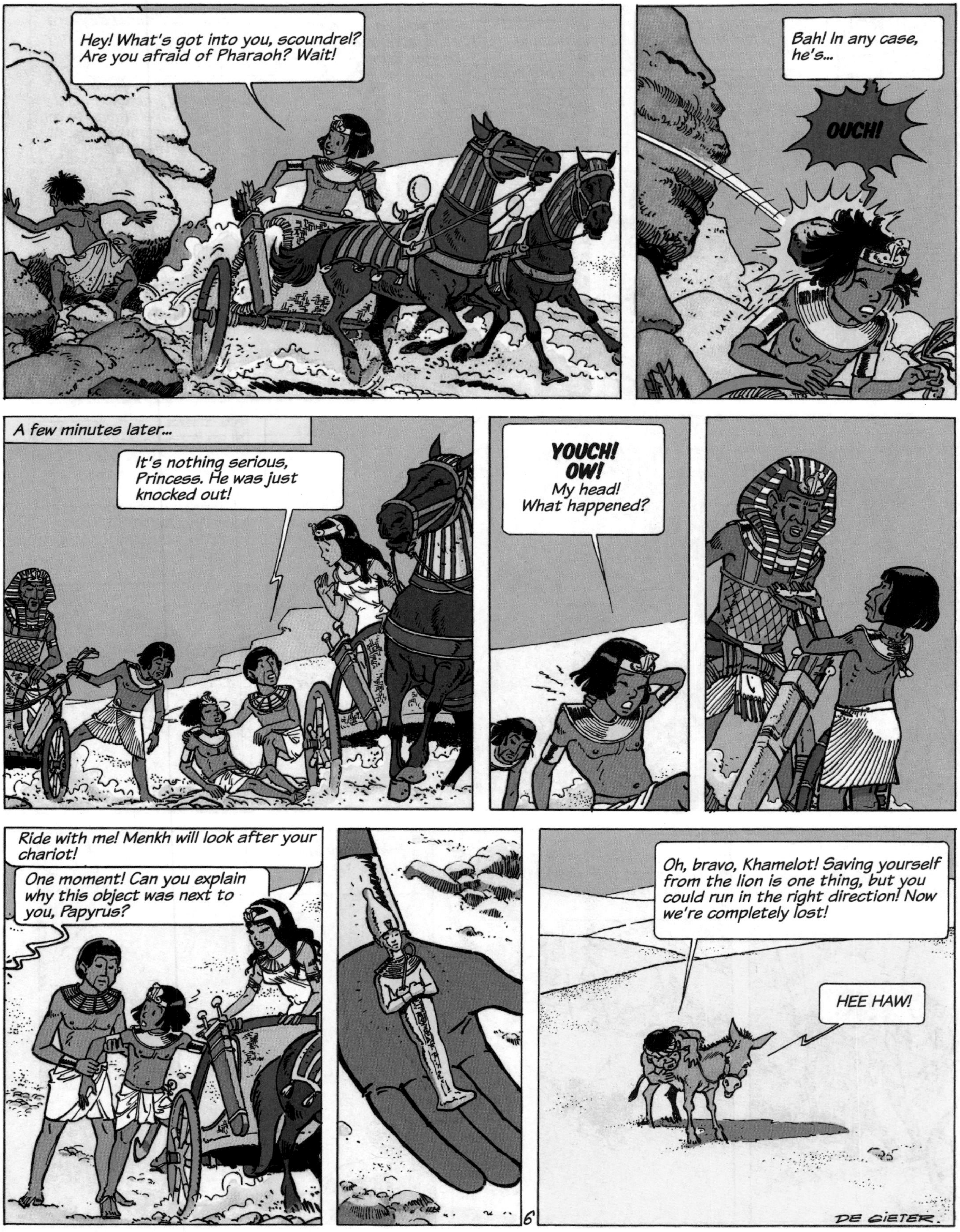
Hey! What's got into you, scoundrel? Are you afraid of Pharaoh? Wait!
Bah! In any case, he's...
OUCH!
A few minutes later...
It's nothing serious, Princess. He was just knocked out!
YOUCH! OW! My head! What happened?
Ride with me! Menkh will look after your chariot!
One moment! Can you explain why this object was next to you, Papyrus?
Oh, bravo, Khamelot! Saving yourself from the lion is one thing, but you could run in the right direction! Now we're completely lost!
HEE HAW!
6
DE GIETER.

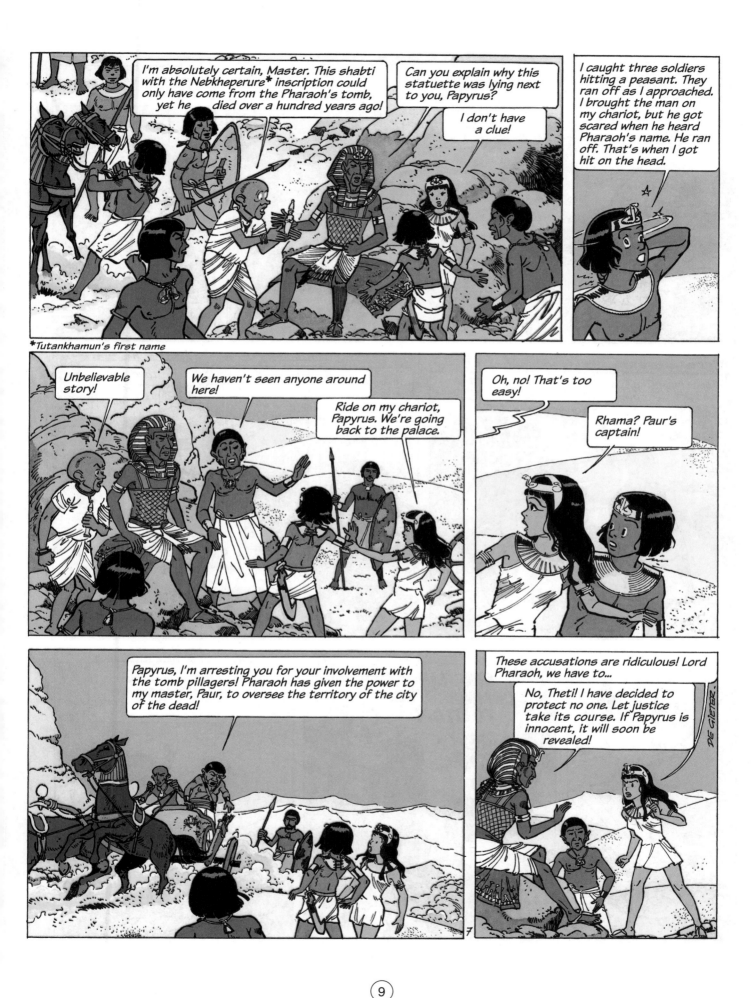

I'm absolutely certain, Master. This shabti with the Nebkheperure* inscription could only have come from the Pharaoh's tomb, yet he died over a hundred years ago!

Can you explain why this statuette was lying next to you, Papyrus?

I don't have a clue!

I caught three soldiers hitting a peasant. They ran off as I approached. I brought the man on my chariot, but he got scared when he heard Pharaoh's name. He ran off. That's when I got hit on the head.

*Tutankhamun's first name

Unbelievable story!

We haven't seen anyone around here!

Ride on my chariot, Papyrus. We're going back to the palace.

Oh, no! That's too easy!

Rhama? Paur's captain!

Papyrus, I'm arresting you for your involvement with the tomb pillagers! Pharaoh has given the power to my master, Paur, to oversee the territory of the city of the dead!

These accusations are ridiculous! Lord Pharaoh, we have to...

No, Theti! I have decided to protect no one. Let justice take its course. If Papyrus is innocent, it will soon be revealed!

7

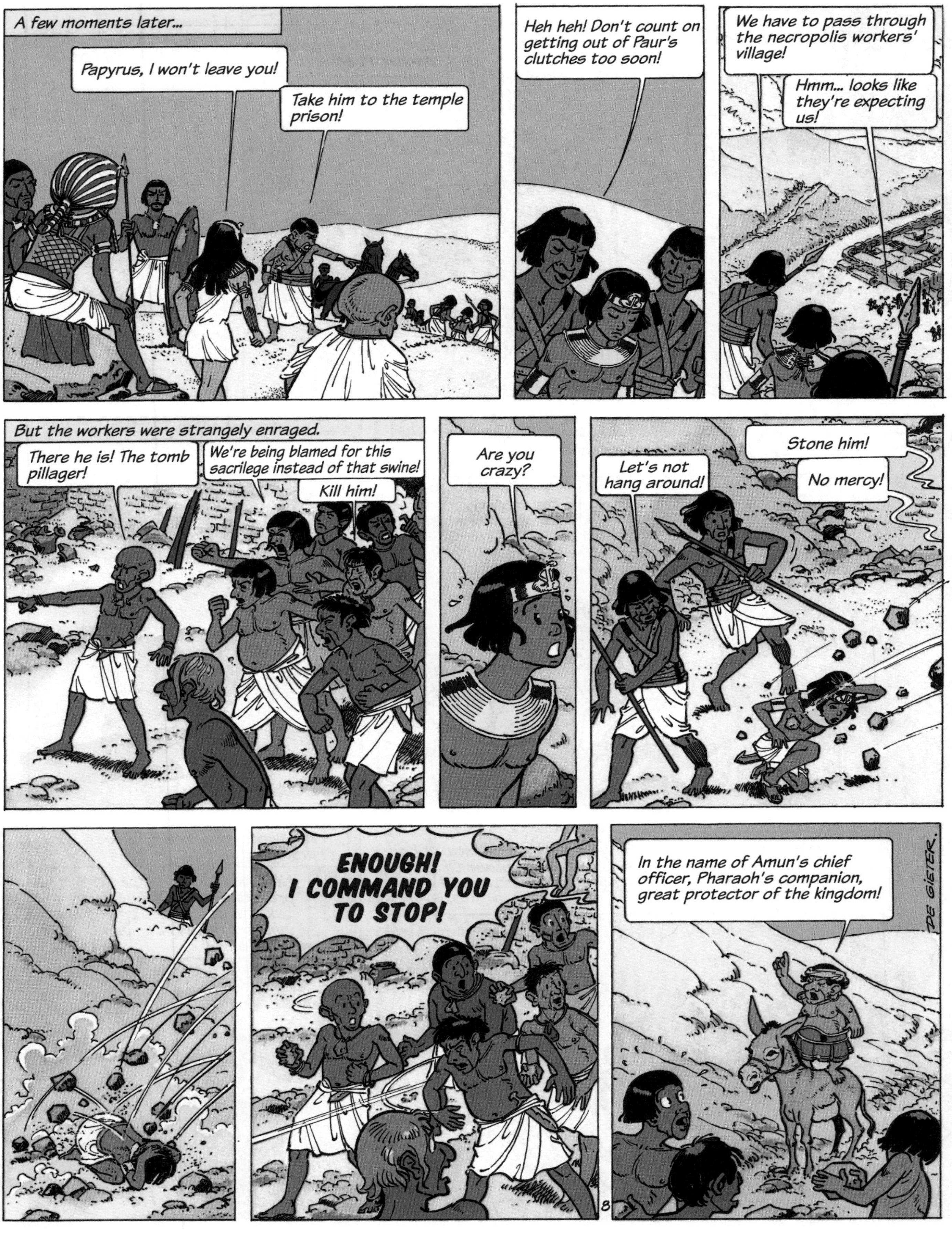
A few moments later...
Papyrus, I won't leave you!
Take him to the temple prison!
Heh heh! Don't count on getting out of Paur's clutches too soon!
We have to pass through the necropolis workers' village!
Hmm... looks like they're expecting us!
But the workers were strangely enraged.
There he is! The tomb pillager!
We're being blamed for this sacrilege instead of that swine!
Kill him!
Are you crazy?
Let's not hang around!
Stone him!
No mercy!
ENOUGH! I COMMAND YOU TO STOP!
In the name of Amun's chief officer, Pharaoh's companion, great protector of the kingdom!
DE GIETER
8

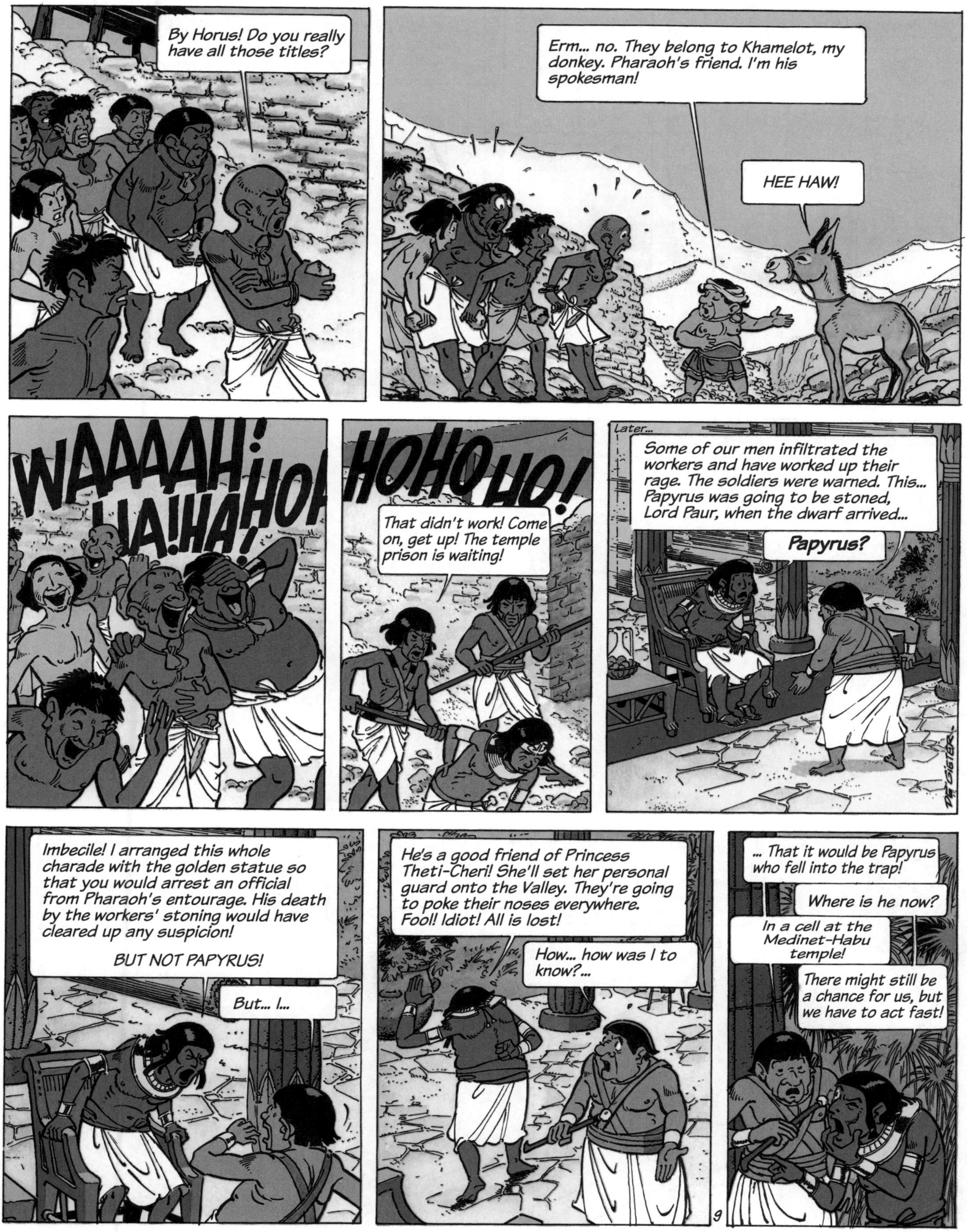

By Horus! Do you really have all those titles?
Erm... no. They belong to Khamelot, my donkey. Pharaoh's friend. I'm his spokesman!
HEE HAW!
WAAAAH! HA!HA! HO! HOHOHO HO!
That didn't work! Come on, get up! The temple prison is waiting!
Later...
Some of our men infiltrated the workers and have worked up their rage. The soldiers were warned. This... Papyrus was going to be stoned, Lord Paur, when the dwarf arrived...
Papyrus?
Imbecile! I arranged this whole charade with the golden statue so that you would arrest an official from Pharaoh's entourage. His death by the workers' stoning would have cleared up any suspicion!
BUT NOT PAPYRUS!
But... I...
He's a good friend of Princess Theti-Cheri! She'll set her personal guard onto the Valley. They're going to poke their noses everywhere. Fool! Idiot! All is lost!
How... how was I to know?...
... That it would be Papyrus who fell into the trap!
Where is he now?
In a cell at the Medinet-Habu temple!
There might still be a chance for us, but we have to act fast!
9

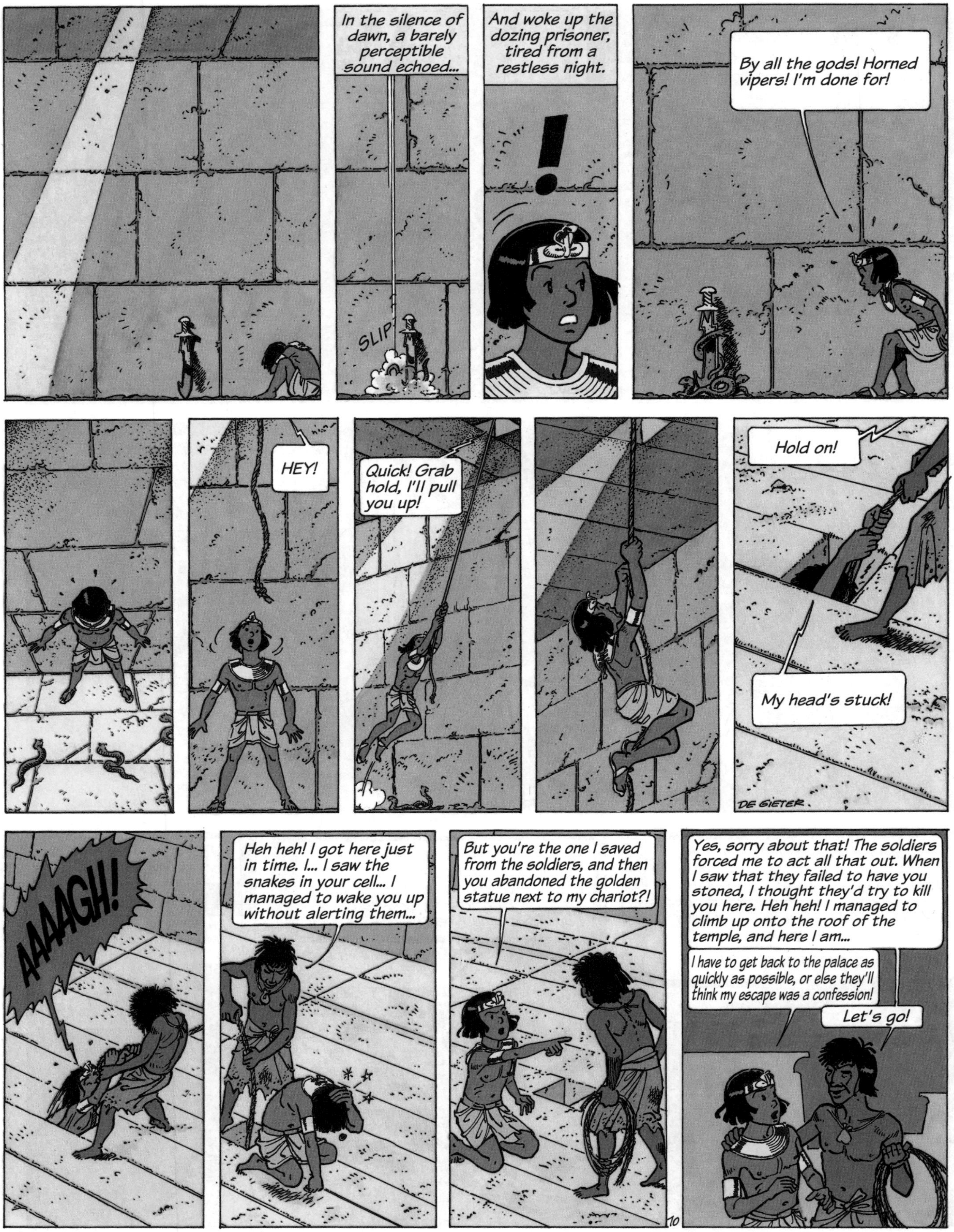
In the silence of dawn, a barely perceptible sound echoed...
SLIP
And woke up the dozing prisoner, tired from a restless night.
!
By all the gods! Horned vipers! I'm done for!
HEY!
Quick! Grab hold, I'll pull you up!
Hold on!
My head's stuck!
DE GIETER
AAAAGH!
Heh heh! I got here just in time. I... I saw the snakes in your cell... I managed to wake you up without alerting them...
But you're the one I saved from the soldiers, and then you abandoned the golden statue next to my chariot?!
Yes, sorry about that! The soldiers forced me to act all that out. When I saw that they failed to have you stoned, I thought they'd try to kill you here. Heh heh! I managed to climb up onto the roof of the temple, and here I am...
I have to get back to the palace as quickly as possible, or else they'll think my escape was a confession!
Let's go!
10

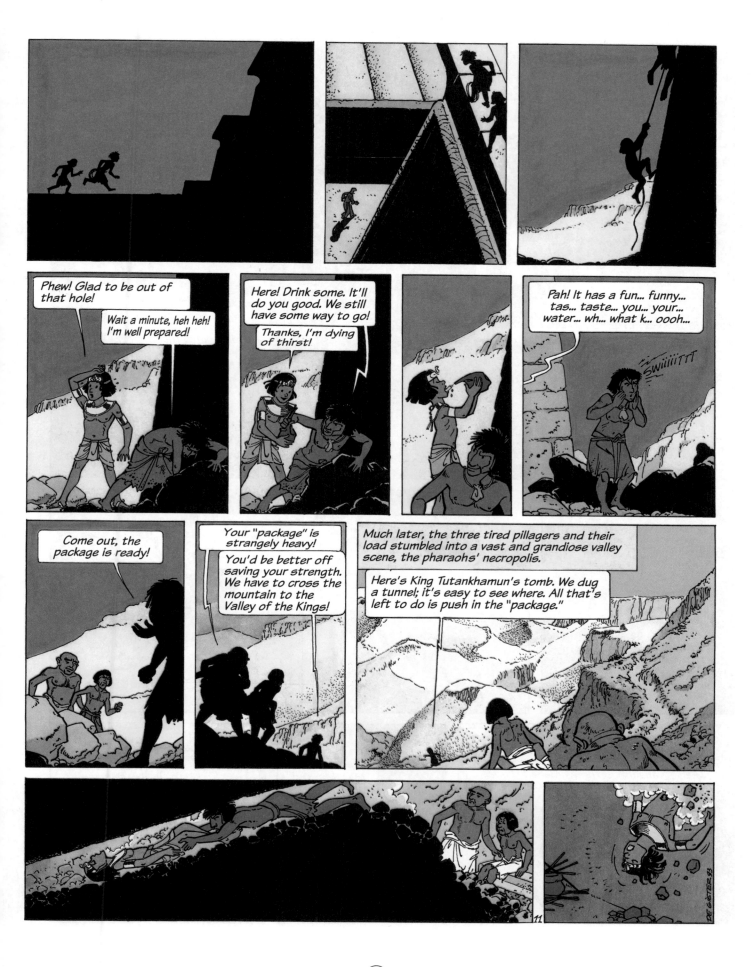

Phew! Glad to be out of that hole!

Wait a minute, heh heh! I'm well prepared!

Here! Drink some. It'll do you good. We still have some way to go!

Thanks, I'm dying of thirst!

Pah! It has a fun... funny... tas... taste... you... your... water... wh... what k... oooh...

Swiiiiittt

Come out, the package is ready!

Your "package" is strangely heavy!

You'd be better off saving your strength. We have to cross the mountain to the Valley of the Kings!

Much later, the three tired pillagers and their load stumbled into a vast and grandiose valley scene, the pharaohs' necropolis.

Here's King Tutankhamun's tomb. We dug a tunnel; it's easy to see where. All that's left to do is push in the "package."

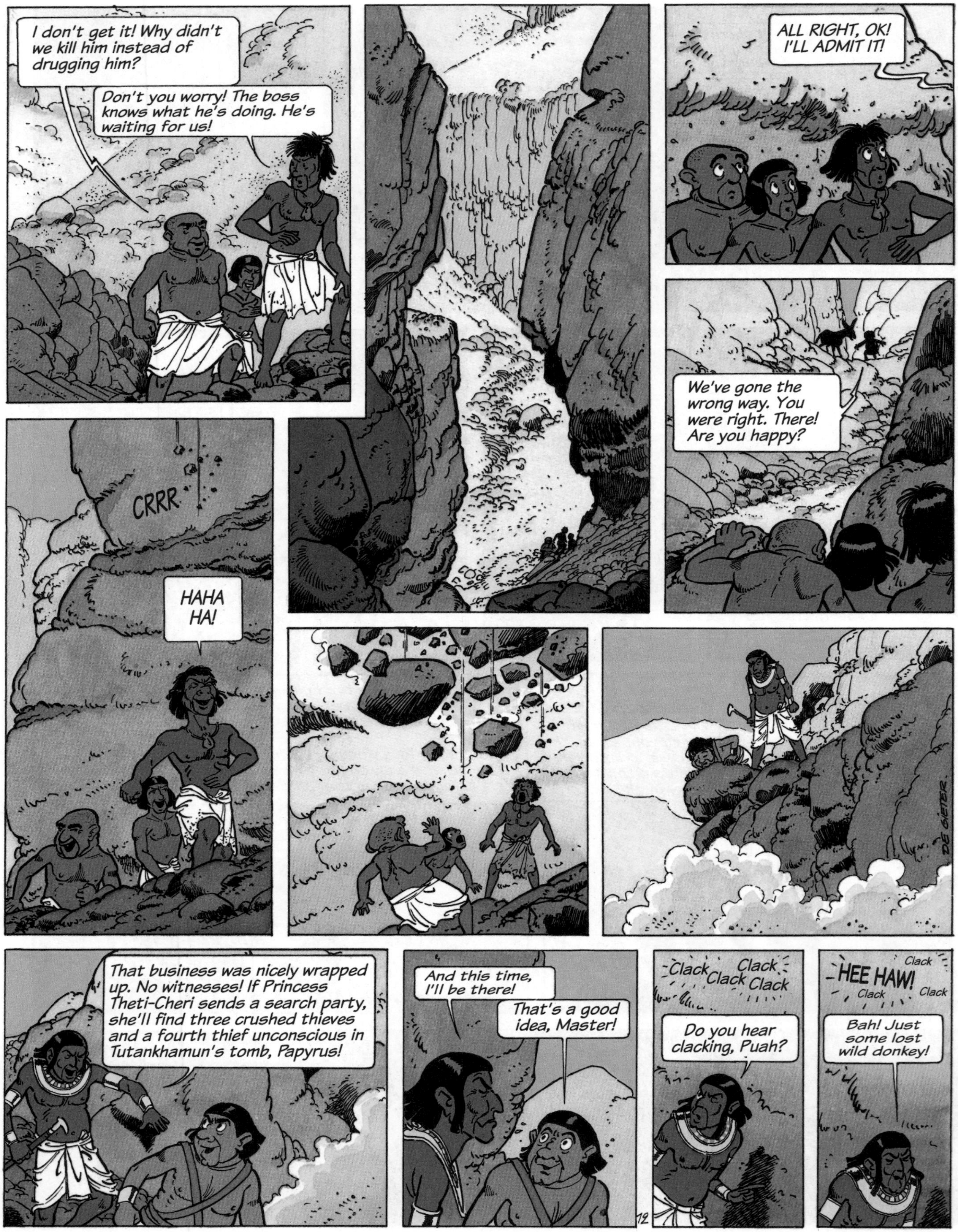
I don't get it! Why didn't we kill him instead of drugging him?
Don't you worry! The boss knows what he's doing. He's waiting for us!
ALL RIGHT, OK! I'LL ADMIT IT!
We've gone the wrong way. You were right. There! Are you happy?
CRRR
HAHA HA!
DE GIETER
That business was nicely wrapped up. No witnesses! If Princess Theti-Cheri sends a search party, she'll find three crushed thieves and a fourth thief unconscious in Tutankhamun's tomb, Papyrus!
And this time, I'll be there!
That's a good idea, Master!
Clack Clack Clack Clack
Do you hear clacking, Puah?
HEE HAW! Clack Clack Clack
Bah! Just some lost wild donkey!
12

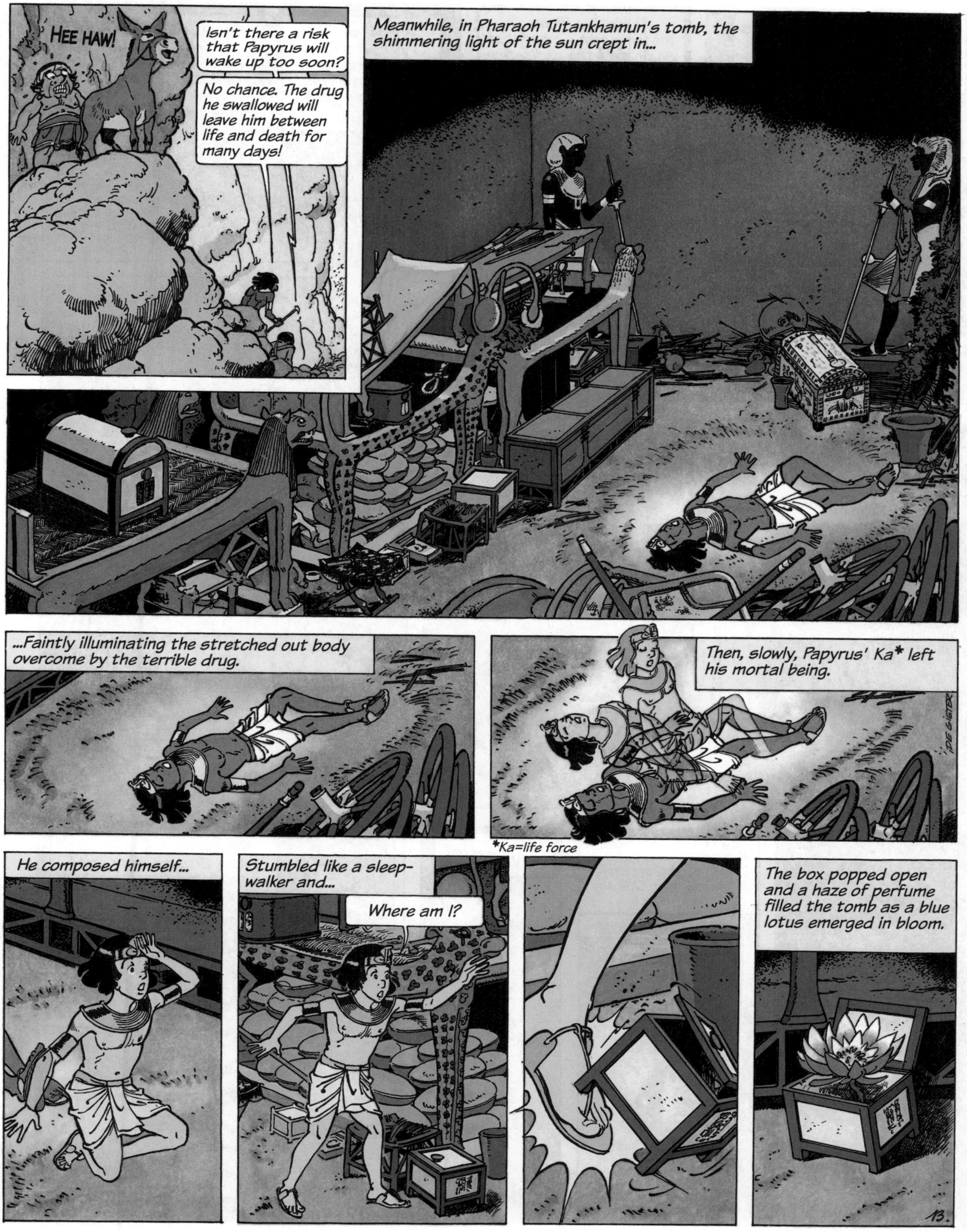
HEE HAW!
Isn't there a risk that Papyrus will wake up too soon?
No chance. The drug he swallowed will leave him between life and death for many days!
Meanwhile, in Pharaoh Tutankhamun's tomb, the shimmering light of the sun crept in...
...Faintly illuminating the stretched out body overcome by the terrible drug.
Then, slowly, Papyrus' Ka* left his mortal being.
DE GIETER
*Ka=life force
He composed himself...
Stumbled like a sleep-walker and...
Where am I?
The box popped open and a haze of perfume filled the tomb as a blue lotus emerged in bloom.
13.

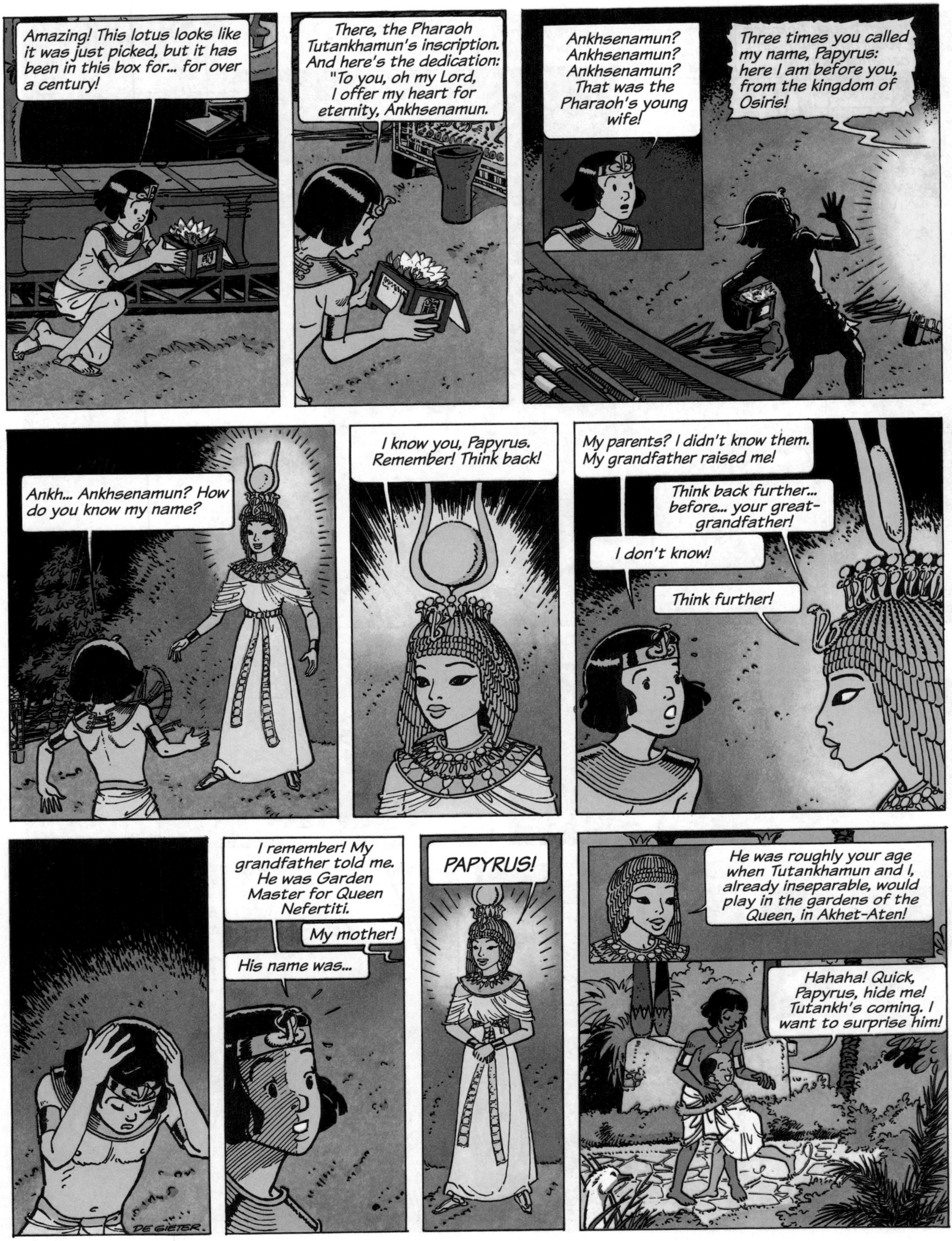
Amazing! This lotus looks like it was just picked, but it has been in this box for... for over a century!
There, the Pharaoh Tutankhamun's inscription. And here's the dedication: "To you, oh my Lord, I offer my heart for eternity, Ankhsenamun.
Ankhsenamun? Ankhsenamun? Ankhsenamun? That was the Pharaoh's young wife!
Three times you called my name, Papyrus: here I am before you, from the kingdom of Osiris!
Ankh... Ankhsenamun? How do you know my name?
I know you, Papyrus. Remember! Think back!
My parents? I didn't know them. My grandfather raised me!
Think back further... before... your great-grandfather!
I don't know!
Think further!
I remember! My grandfather told me. He was Garden Master for Queen Nefertiti.
My mother!
His name was...
PAPYRUS!
He was roughly your age when Tutankhamun and I, already inseparable, would play in the gardens of the Queen, in Akhet-Aten!
Hahaha! Quick, Papyrus, hide me! Tutankh's coming. I want to surprise him!
DE GIETER

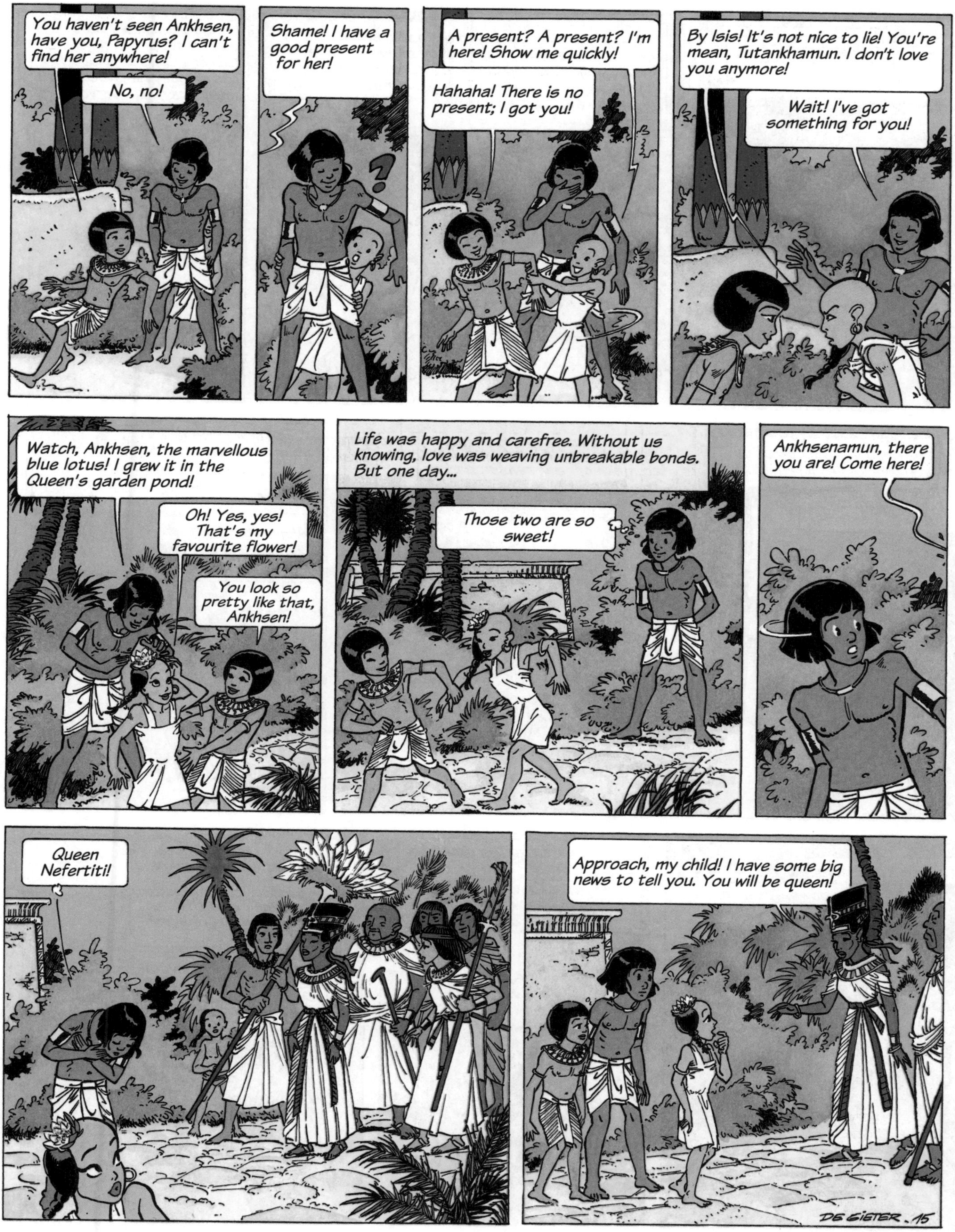
You haven't seen Ankhsen, have you, Papyrus? I can't find her anywhere!
No, no!
Shame! I have a good present for her!
A present? A present? I'm here! Show me quickly!
Hahaha! There is no present; I got you!
By Isis! It's not nice to lie! You're mean, Tutankhamun. I don't love you anymore!
Wait! I've got something for you!
Watch, Ankhsen, the marvellous blue lotus! I grew it in the Queen's garden pond!
Oh! Yes, yes! That's my favourite flower!
You look so pretty like that, Ankhsen!
Life was happy and carefree. Without us knowing, love was weaving unbreakable bonds. But one day...
Those two are so sweet!
Ankhsenamun, there you are! Come here!
Queen Nefertiti!
Approach, my child! I have some big news to tell you. You will be queen!
DE GIETER . 15

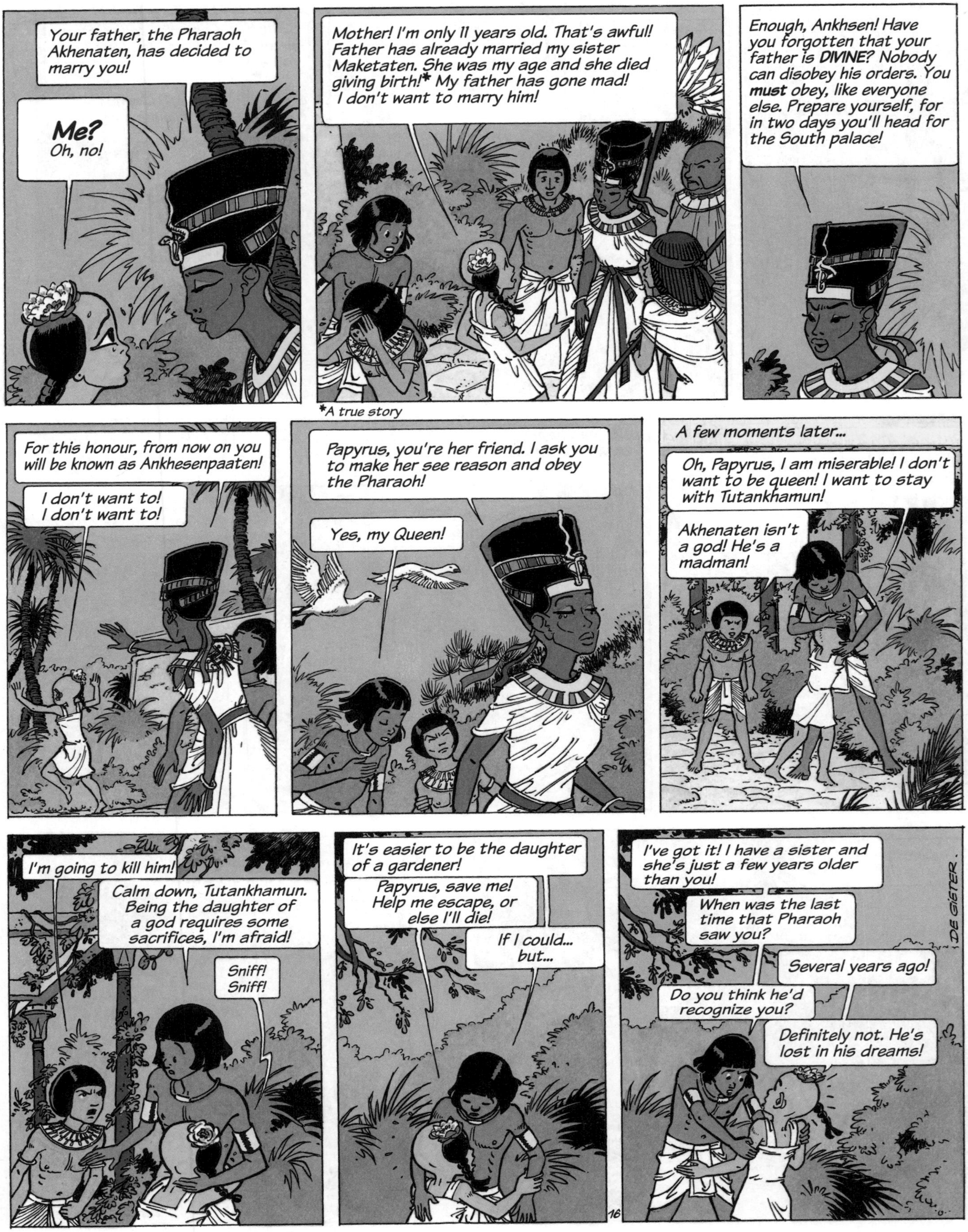

Your father, the Pharaoh Akhenaten, has decided to marry you!
Me? Oh, no!
Mother! I'm only 11 years old. That's awful! Father has already married my sister Maketaten. She was my age and she died giving birth!* My father has gone mad! I don't want to marry him!
Enough, Ankhsen! Have you forgotten that your father is **DIVINE**? Nobody can disobey his orders. You **must** obey, like everyone else. Prepare yourself, for in two days you'll head for the South palace!
*A true story
For this honour, from now on you will be known as Ankhesenpaaten!
I don't want to! I don't want to!
Papyrus, you're her friend. I ask you to make her see reason and obey the Pharaoh!
Yes, my Queen!
A few moments later...
Oh, Papyrus, I am miserable! I don't want to be queen! I want to stay with Tutankhamun!
Akhenaten isn't a god! He's a madman!
I'm going to kill him!
Calm down, Tutankhamun. Being the daughter of a god requires some sacrifices, I'm afraid!
Sniff! Sniff!
It's easier to be the daughter of a gardener!
Papyrus, save me! Help me escape, or else I'll die!
If I could... but...
16
I've got it! I have a sister and she's just a few years older than you!
When was the last time that Pharaoh saw you?
Several years ago!
Do you think he'd recognize you?
Definitely not. He's lost in his dreams!
DE GIETER

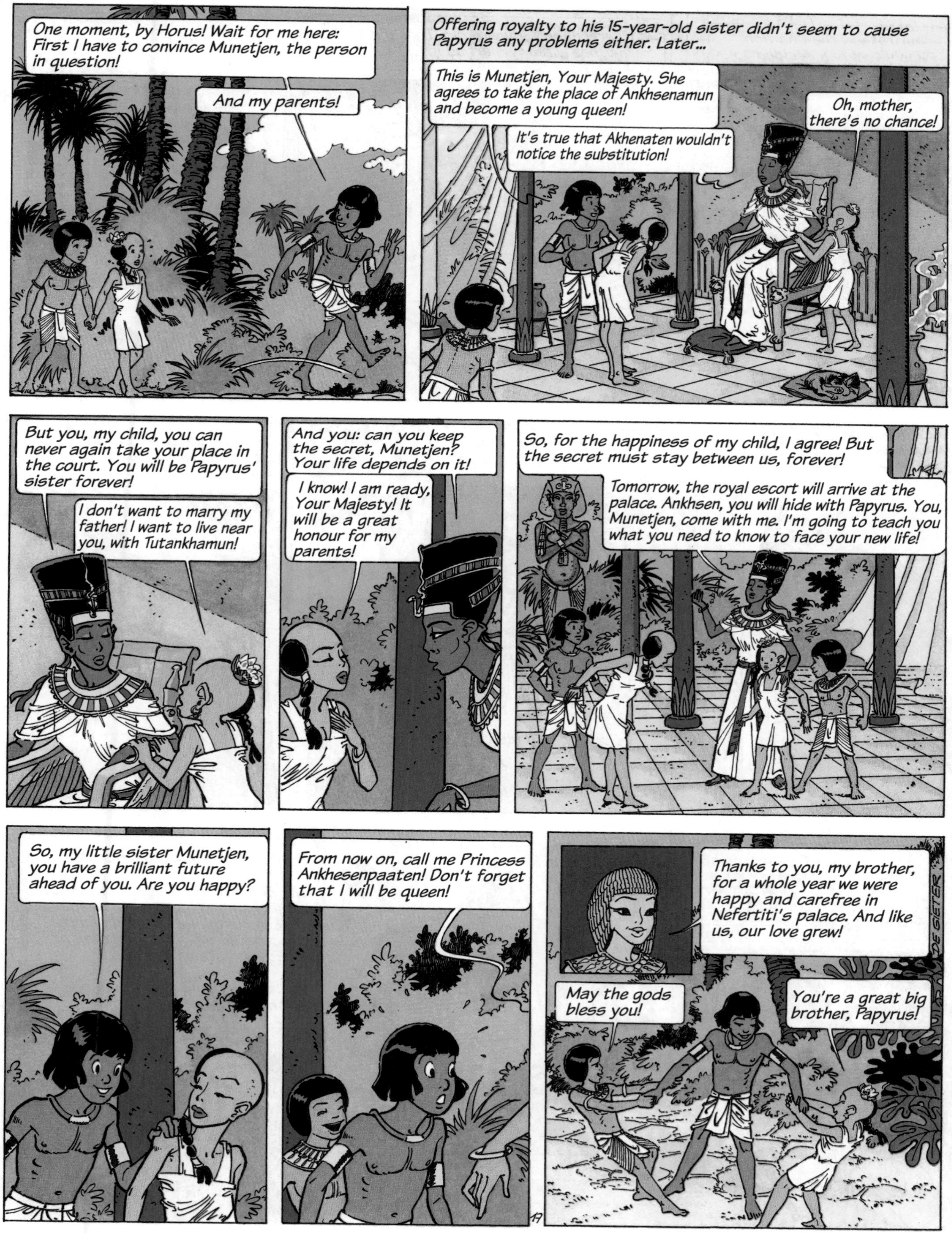
One moment, by Horus! Wait for me here: First I have to convince Munetjen, the person in question!
And my parents!
Offering royalty to his 15-year-old sister didn't seem to cause Papyrus any problems either. Later...
This is Munetjen, Your Majesty. She agrees to take the place of Ankhsenamun and become a young queen!
It's true that Akhenaten wouldn't notice the substitution!
Oh, mother, there's no chance!
But you, my child, you can never again take your place in the court. You will be Papyrus' sister forever!
I don't want to marry my father! I want to live near you, with Tutankhamun!
And you: can you keep the secret, Munetjen? Your life depends on it!
I know! I am ready, Your Majesty! It will be a great honour for my parents!
So, for the happiness of my child, I agree! But the secret must stay between us, forever!
Tomorrow, the royal escort will arrive at the palace. Ankhsen, you will hide with Papyrus. You, Munetjen, come with me. I'm going to teach you what you need to know to face your new life!
So, my little sister Munetjen, you have a brilliant future ahead of you. Are you happy?
From now on, call me Princess Ankhesenpaaten! Don't forget that I will be queen!
Thanks to you, my brother, for a whole year we were happy and carefree in Nefertiti's palace. And like us, our love grew!
May the gods bless you!
You're a great big brother, Papyrus!
DE GIETER

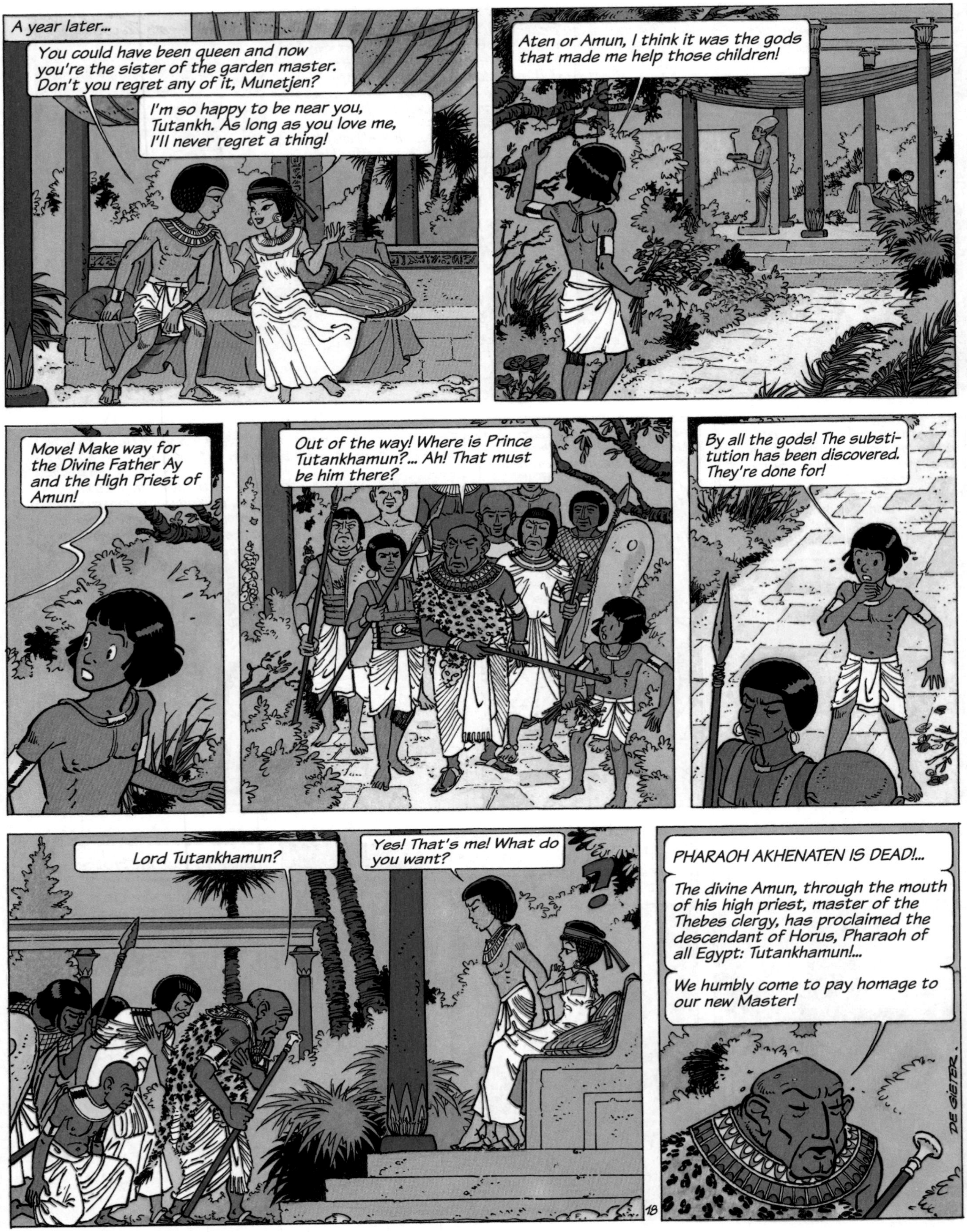

A year later...
You could have been queen and now you're the sister of the garden master. Don't you regret any of it, Munetjen?
I'm so happy to be near you, Tutankh. As long as you love me, I'll never regret a thing!
Aten or Amun, I think it was the gods that made me help those children!
Move! Make way for the Divine Father Ay and the High Priest of Amun!
Out of the way! Where is Prince Tutankhamun?... Ah! That must be him there?
By all the gods! The substitution has been discovered. They're done for!
Lord Tutankhamun?
Yes! That's me! What do you want?
?
PHARAOH AKHENATEN IS DEAD!...
The divine Amun, through the mouth of his high priest, master of the Thebes clergy, has proclaimed the descendant of Horus, Pharaoh of all Egypt: Tutankhamun!...
We humbly come to pay homage to our new Master!
DE GIETER.
18

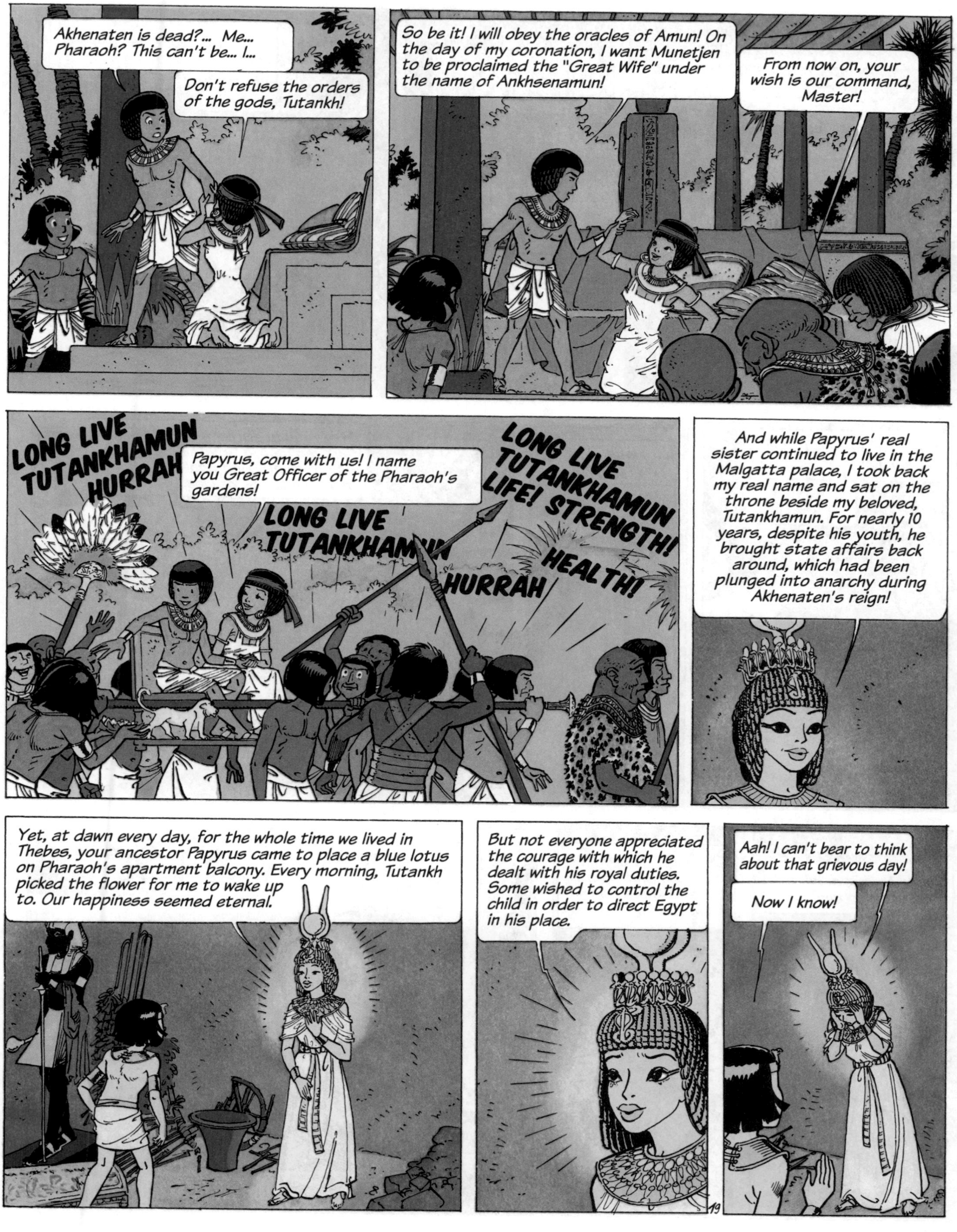
Akhenaten is dead?... Me... Pharaoh? This can't be... I...
Don't refuse the orders of the gods, Tutankh!
So be it! I will obey the oracles of Amun! On the day of my coronation, I want Munetjen to be proclaimed the "Great Wife" under the name of Ankhsenamun!
From now on, your wish is our command, Master!
LONG LIVE TUTANKHAMUN HURRAH
Papyrus, come with us! I name you Great Officer of the Pharaoh's gardens!
LONG LIVE TUTANKHAMUN
LONG LIVE TUTANKHAMUN LIFE! STRENGTH!
HEALTH!
HURRAH
And while Papyrus' real sister continued to live in the Malgatta palace, I took back my real name and sat on the throne beside my beloved, Tutankhamun. For nearly 10 years, despite his youth, he brought state affairs back around, which had been plunged into anarchy during Akhenaten's reign!
Yet, at dawn every day, for the whole time we lived in Thebes, your ancestor Papyrus came to place a blue lotus on Pharaoh's apartment balcony. Every morning, Tutankh picked the flower for me to wake up to. Our happiness seemed eternal.
But not everyone appreciated the courage with which he dealt with his royal duties. Some wished to control the child in order to direct Egypt in his place.
Aah! I can't bear to think about that grievous day!
Now I know!
19

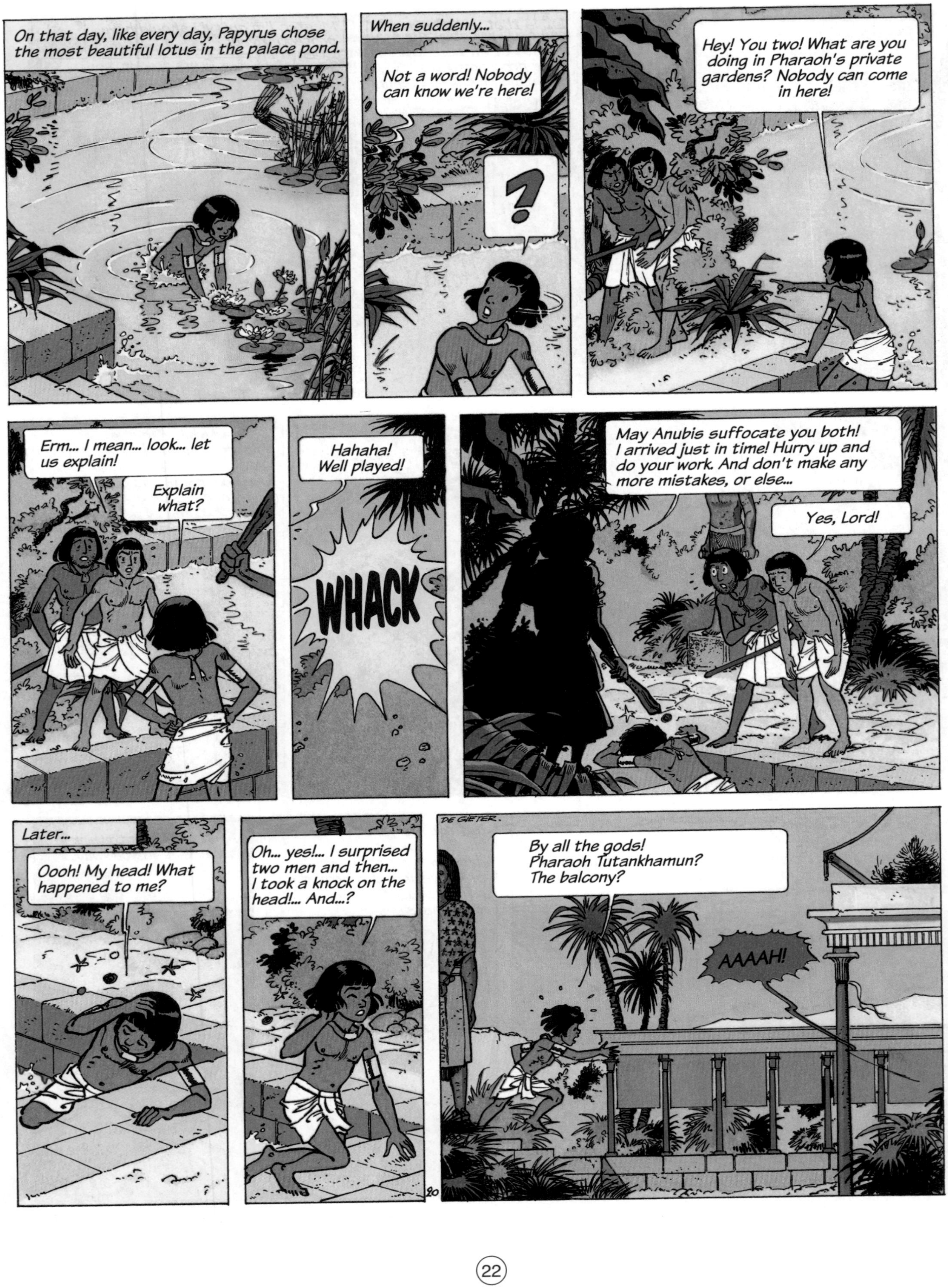

On that day, like every day, Papyrus chose the most beautiful lotus in the palace pond.
When suddenly...
Not a word! Nobody can know we're here!
?
Hey! You two! What are you doing in Pharaoh's private gardens? Nobody can come in here!
Erm... I mean... look... let us explain!
Explain what?
Hahaha! Well played!
WHACK
May Anubis suffocate you both! I arrived just in time! Hurry up and do your work. And don't make any more mistakes, or else...
Yes, Lord!
Later...
Oooh! My head! What happened to me?
Oh... yes!... I surprised two men and then... I took a knock on the head!... And...?
By all the gods! Pharaoh Tutankhamun? The balcony?
AAAAH!

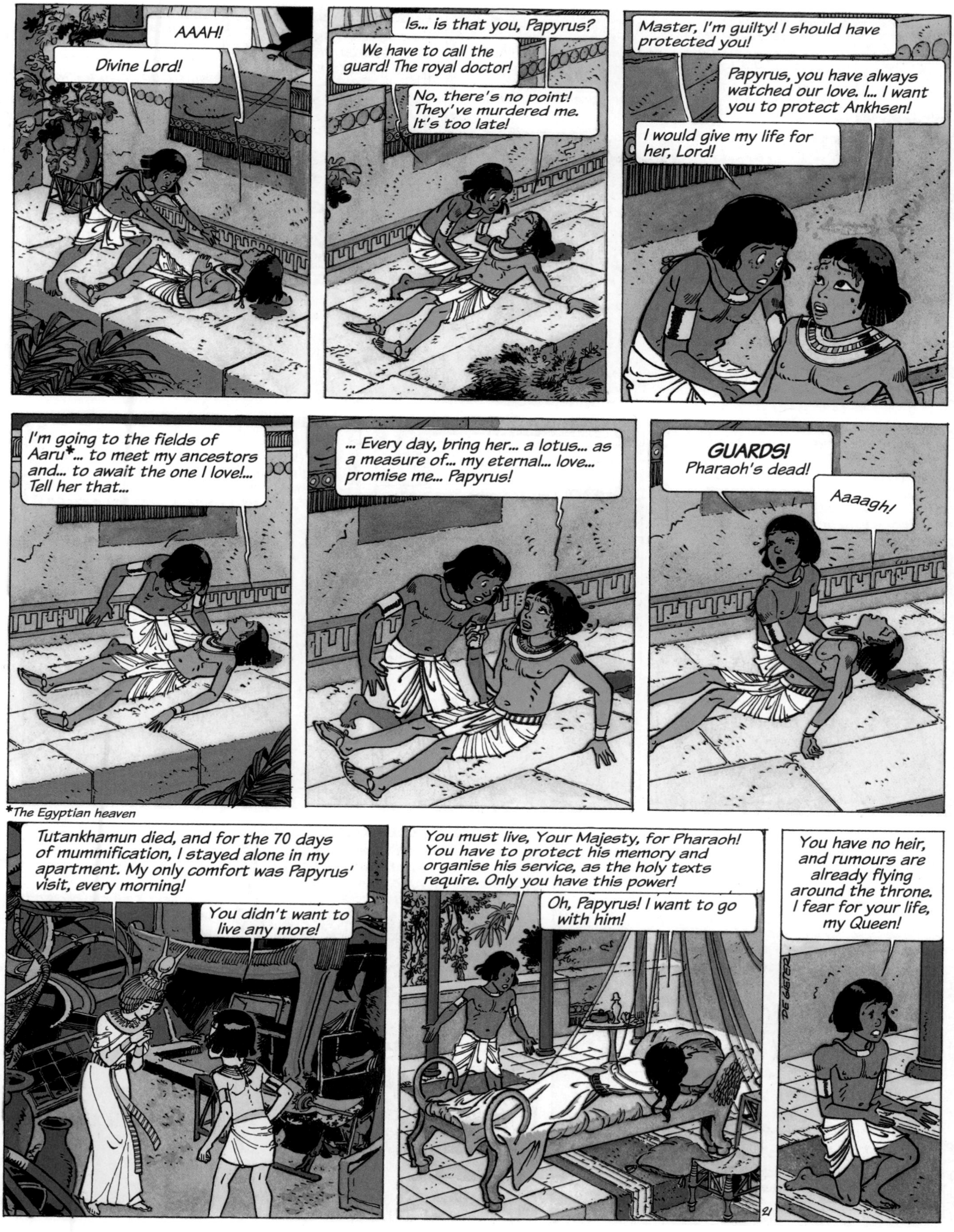
AAAH!
Divine Lord!
Is... is that you, Papyrus?
We have to call the guard! The royal doctor!
No, there's no point! They've murdered me. It's too late!
Master, I'm guilty! I should have protected you!
Papyrus, you have always watched our love. I... I want you to protect Ankhsen!
I would give my life for her, Lord!
I'm going to the fields of Aaru*... to meet my ancestors and... to await the one I love!... Tell her that...
... Every day, bring her... a lotus... as a measure of... my eternal... love... promise me... Papyrus!
GUARDS! Pharaoh's dead!
Aaaagh!
Tutankhamun died, and for the 70 days of mummification, I stayed alone in my apartment. My only comfort was Papyrus' visit, every morning!
You didn't want to live any more!
You must live, Your Majesty, for Pharaoh! You have to protect his memory and organise his service, as the holy texts require. Only you have this power!
Oh, Papyrus! I want to go with him!
You have no heir, and rumours are already flying around the throne. I fear for your life, my Queen!
DE GIETER
21

*The Egyptian heaven

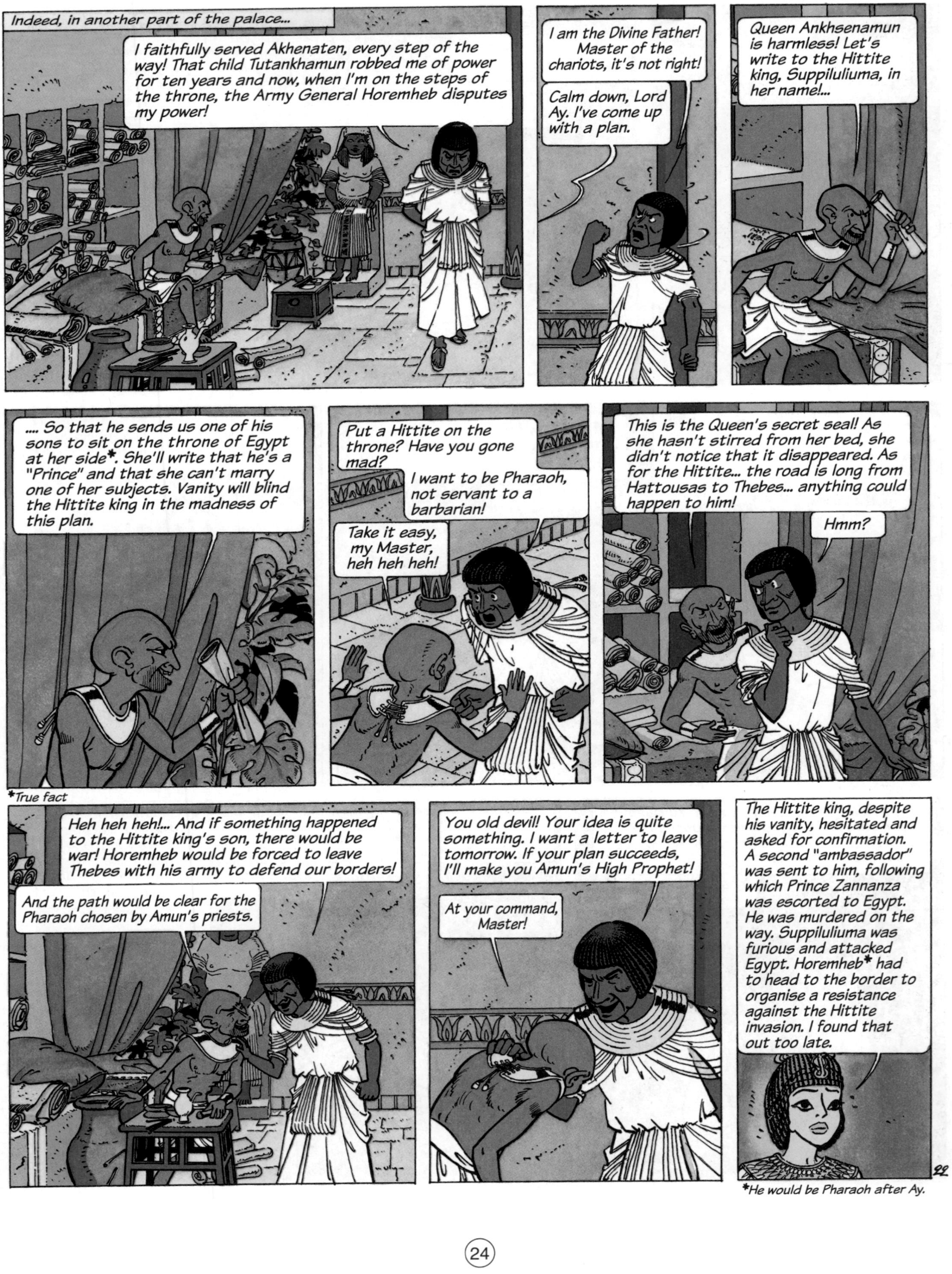

Indeed, in another part of the palace...
I faithfully served Akhenaten, every step of the way! That child Tutankhamun robbed me of power for ten years and now, when I'm on the steps of the throne, the Army General Horemheb disputes my power!
I am the Divine Father! Master of the chariots, it's not right!
Calm down, Lord Ay. I've come up with a plan.
Queen Ankhsenamun is harmless! Let's write to the Hittite king, Suppiluliuma, in her name!...
.... So that he sends us one of his sons to sit on the throne of Egypt at her side*. She'll write that he's a "Prince" and that she can't marry one of her subjects. Vanity will blind the Hittite king in the madness of this plan.
Put a Hittite on the throne? Have you gone mad?
I want to be Pharaoh, not servant to a barbarian!
Take it easy, my Master, heh heh heh!
This is the Queen's secret seal! As she hasn't stirred from her bed, she didn't notice that it disappeared. As for the Hittite... the road is long from Hattousas to Thebes... anything could happen to him!
Hmm?
*True fact
Heh heh heh!... And if something happened to the Hittite king's son, there would be war! Horemheb would be forced to leave Thebes with his army to defend our borders!
And the path would be clear for the Pharaoh chosen by Amun's priests.
You old devil! Your idea is quite something. I want a letter to leave tomorrow. If your plan succeeds, I'll make you Amun's High Prophet!
At your command, Master!
The Hittite king, despite his vanity, hesitated and asked for confirmation. A second "ambassador" was sent to him, following which Prince Zannanza was escorted to Egypt. He was murdered on the way. Suppiluliuma was furious and attacked Egypt. Horemheb* had to head to the border to organise a resistance against the Hittite invasion. I found that out too late.
22
*He would be Pharaoh after Ay.

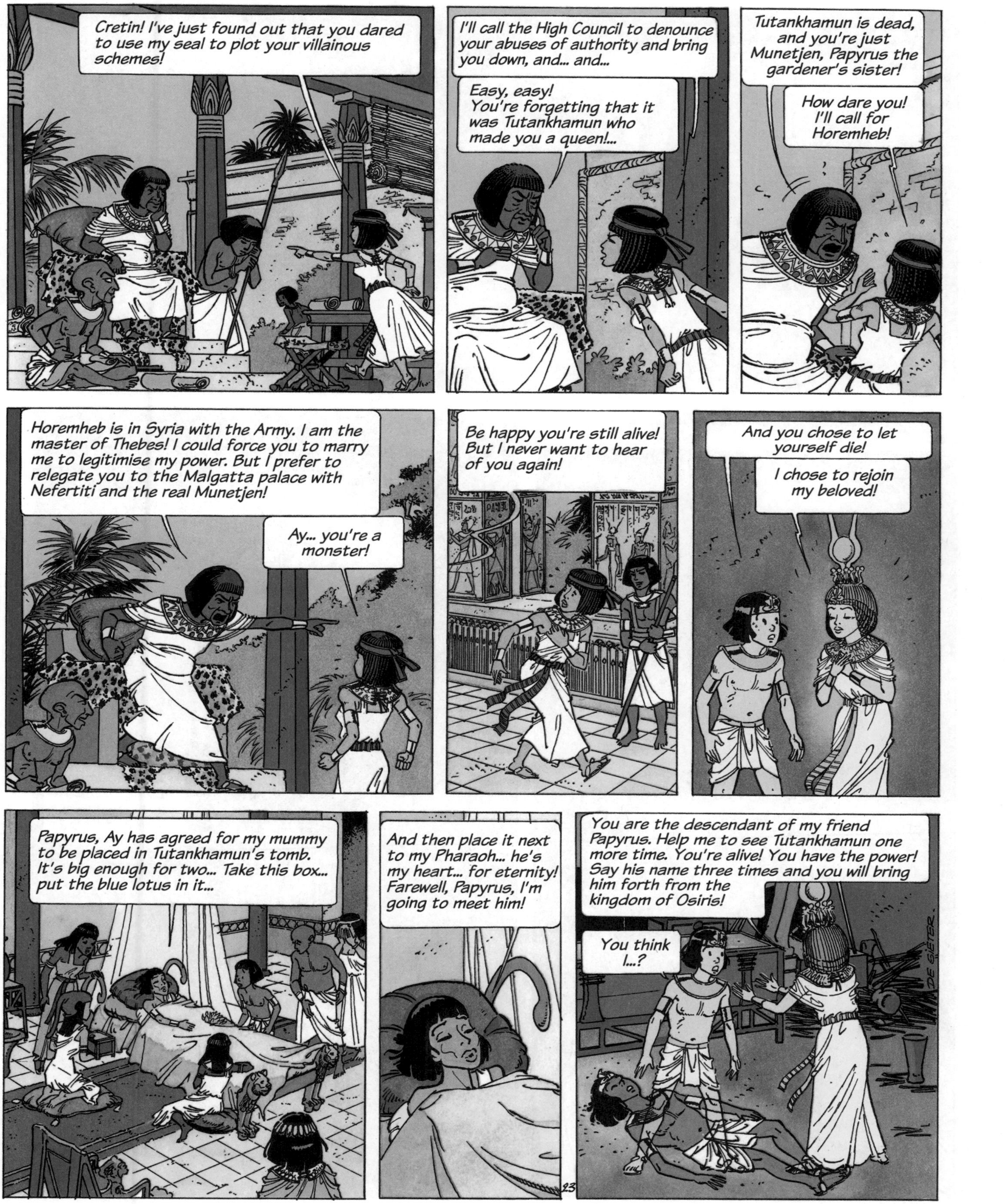
Cretin! I've just found out that you dared to use my seal to plot your villainous schemes!
I'll call the High Council to denounce your abuses of authority and bring you down, and... and...
Easy, easy! You're forgetting that it was Tutankhamun who made you a queen!...
Tutankhamun is dead, and you're just Munetjen, Papyrus the gardener's sister!
How dare you! I'll call for Horemheb!
Horemheb is in Syria with the Army. I am the master of Thebes! I could force you to marry me to legitimise my power. But I prefer to relegate you to the Malgatta palace with Nefertiti and the real Munetjen!
Ay... you're a monster!
Be happy you're still alive! But I never want to hear of you again!
And you chose to let yourself die!
I chose to rejoin my beloved!
Papyrus, Ay has agreed for my mummy to be placed in Tutankhamun's tomb. It's big enough for two... Take this box... put the blue lotus in it...
And then place it next to my Pharaoh... he's my heart... for eternity! Farewell, Papyrus, I'm going to meet him!
You are the descendant of my friend Papyrus. Help me to see Tutankhamun one more time. You're alive! You have the power! Say his name three times and you will bring him forth from the kingdom of Osiris!
You think I...?
DE GIETER
23

So, Papyrus' ka faced the blocked-off funeral chamber and thrice called the name.

TUTANKHAMUN! TUTANKHAMUN! TUTANKHAMUN!

The echo had hardly faded when a vague silhouette slowly emerged from beyond...

By Osiris! Tutankhamun, come to me. I want to see your beloved face!

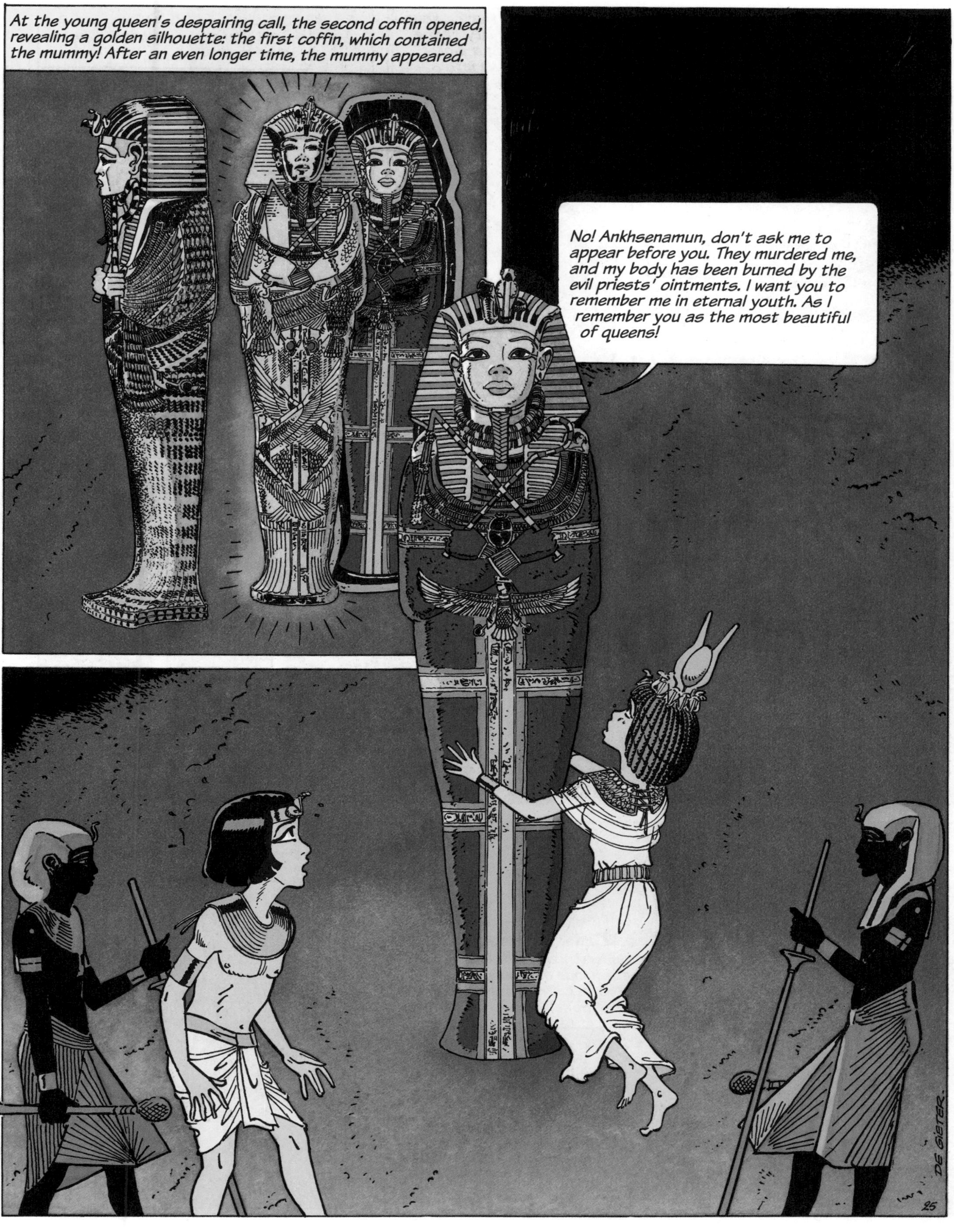

At the young queen's despairing call, the second coffin opened, revealing a golden silhouette: the first coffin, which contained the mummy! After an even longer time, the mummy appeared.
No! Ankhsenamun, don't ask me to appear before you. They murdered me, and my body has been burned by the evil priests' ointments. I want you to remember me in eternal youth. As I remember you as the most beautiful of queens!
DE GIETER.
25

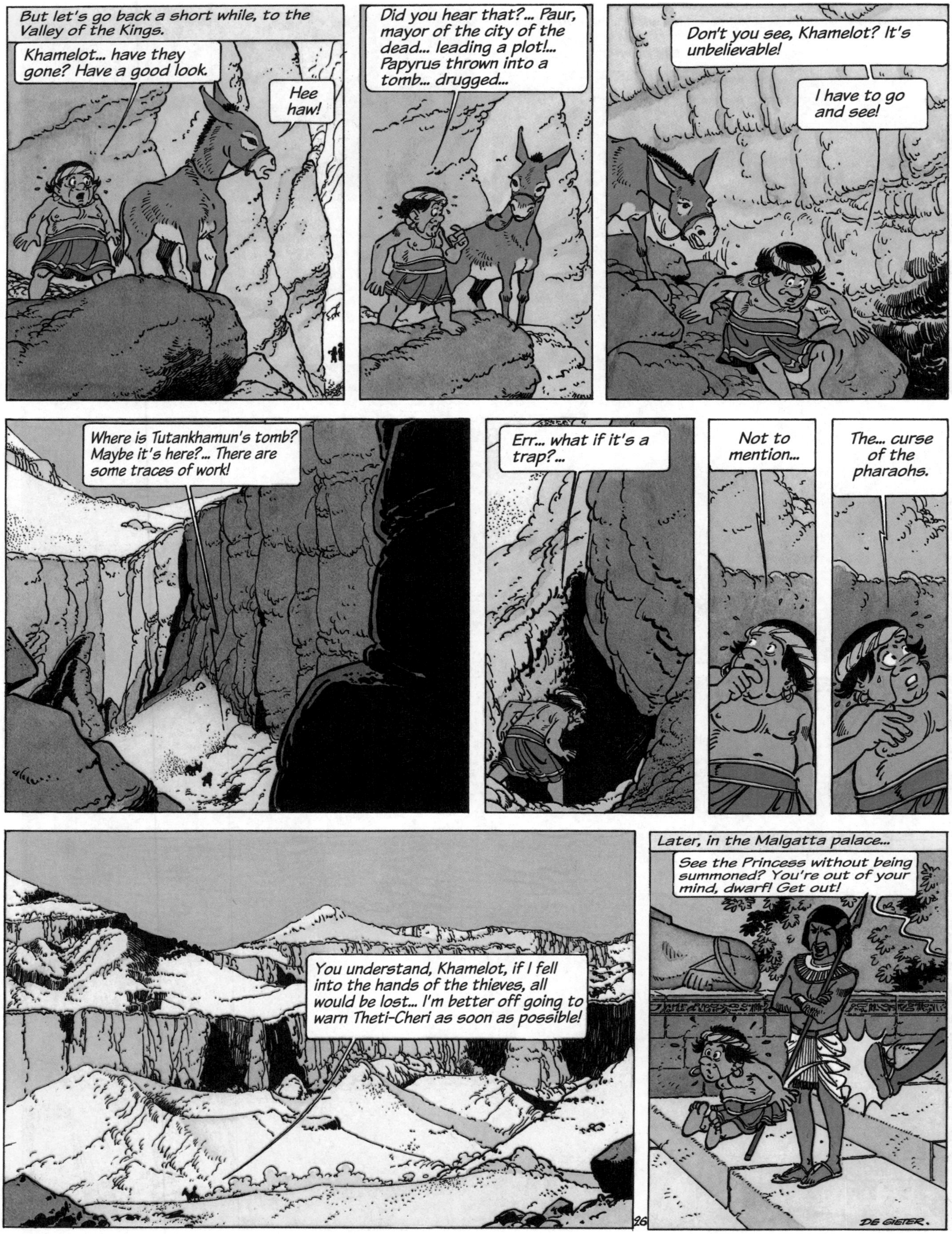
But let's go back a short while, to the Valley of the Kings.
Khamelot... have they gone? Have a good look.
Hee haw!
Did you hear that?... Paur, mayor of the city of the dead... leading a plot!... Papyrus thrown into a tomb... drugged...
Don't you see, Khamelot? It's unbelievable!
I have to go and see!
Where is Tutankhamun's tomb? Maybe it's here?... There are some traces of work!
Err... what if it's a trap?...
Not to mention...
The... curse of the pharaohs.
You understand, Khamelot, if I fell into the hands of the thieves, all would be lost... I'm better off going to warn Theti-Cheri as soon as possible!
Later, in the Malgatta palace...
See the Princess without being summoned? You're out of your mind, dwarf! Get out!
DE GIETER.

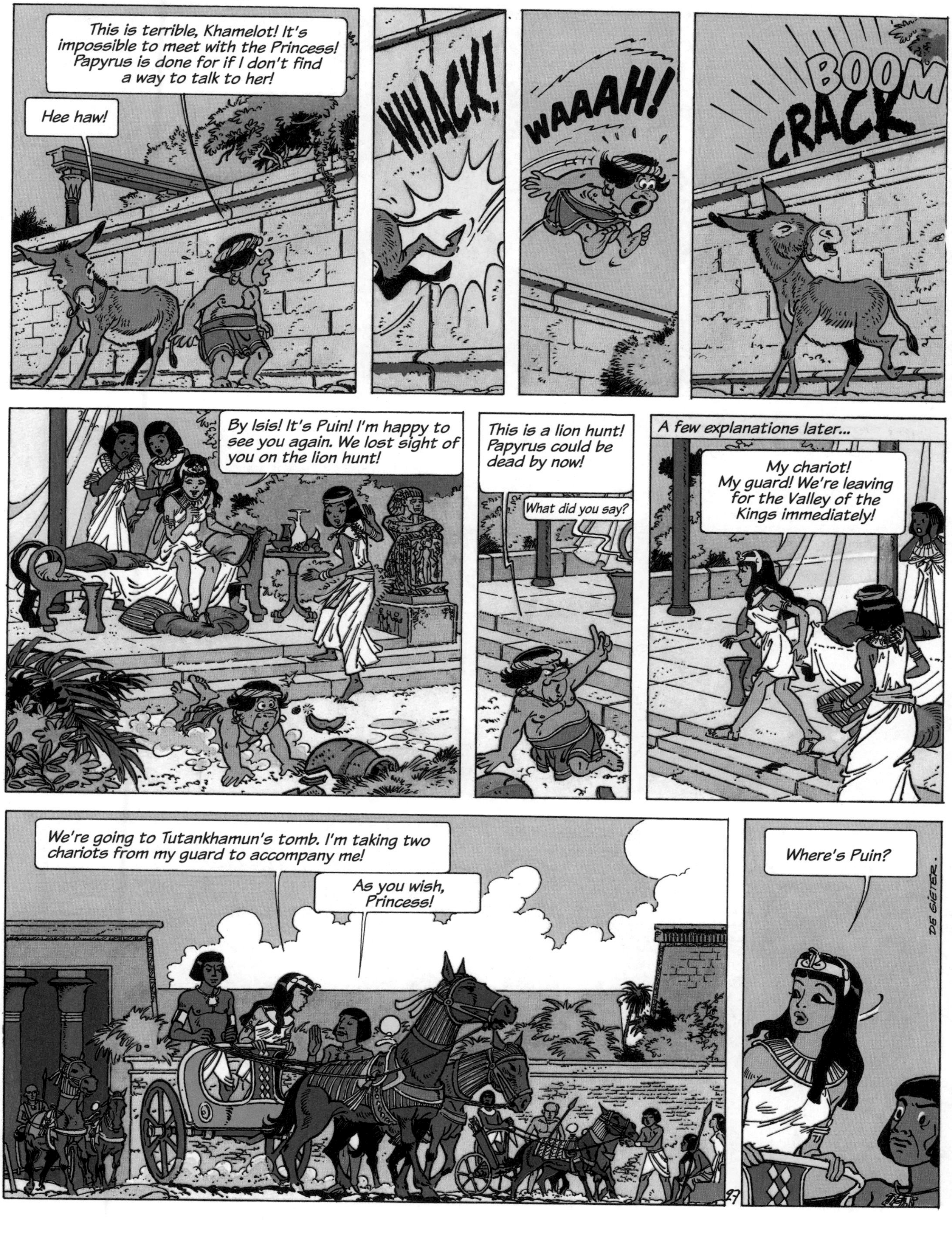

This is terrible, Khamelot! It's impossible to meet with the Princess! Papyrus is done for if I don't find a way to talk to her!
Hee haw!
WHACK!
WAAAH!
BOOM
CRACK
By Isis! It's Puin! I'm happy to see you again. We lost sight of you on the lion hunt!
This is a lion hunt! Papyrus could be dead by now!
What did you say?
A few explanations later...
My chariot! My guard! We're leaving for the Valley of the Kings immediately!
We're going to Tutankhamun's tomb. I'm taking two chariots from my guard to accompany me!
As you wish, Princess!
Where's Puin?
DE GIETER.

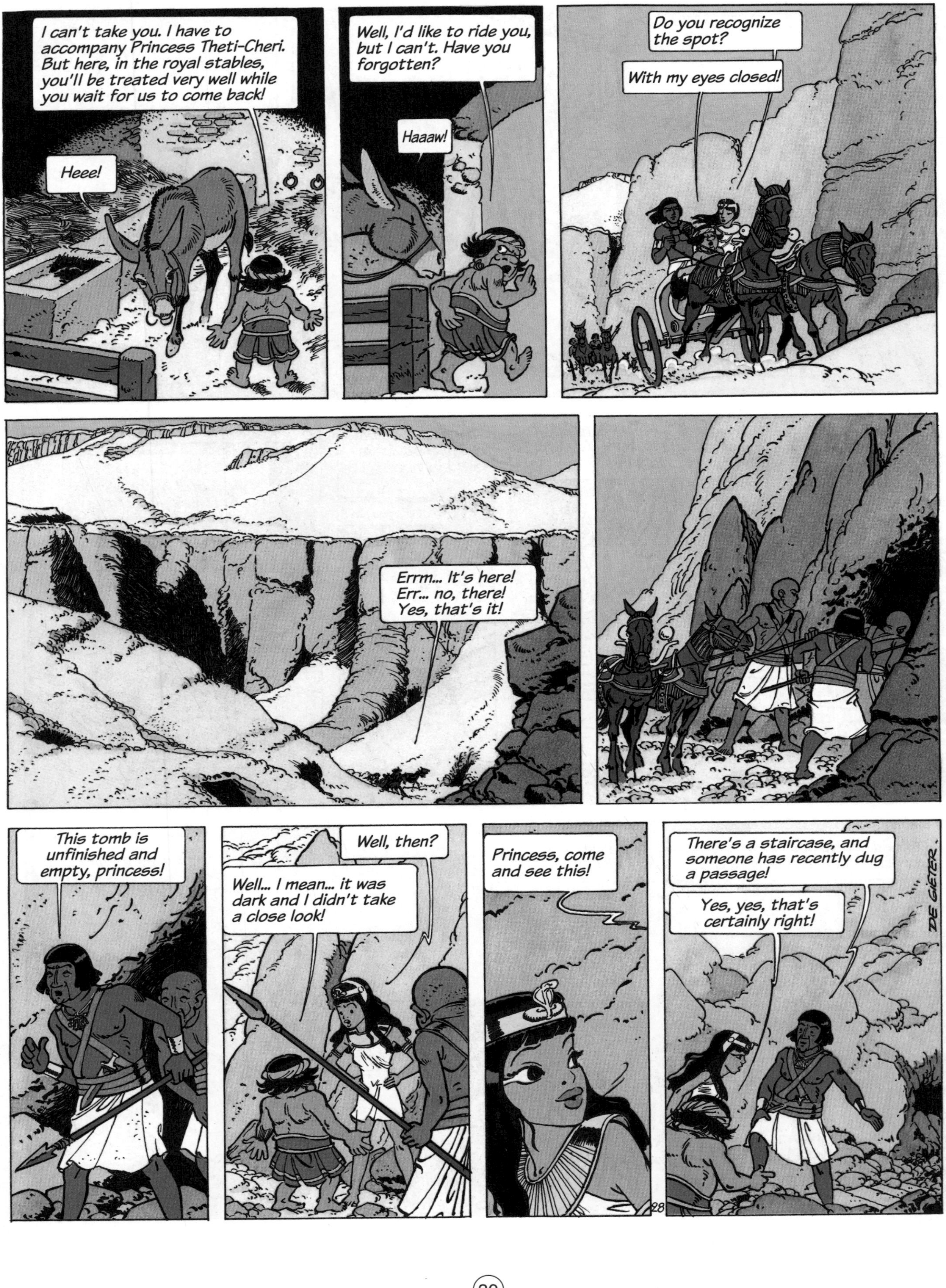
I can't take you. I have to accompany Princess Theti-Cheri. But here, in the royal stables, you'll be treated very well while you wait for us to come back!
Heee!
Well, I'd like to ride you, but I can't. Have you forgotten?
Haaaw!
Do you recognize the spot?
With my eyes closed!
Errm... It's here! Err... no, there! Yes, that's it!
This tomb is unfinished and empty, princess!
Well, then?
Well... I mean... it was dark and I didn't take a close look!
Princess, come and see this!
There's a staircase, and someone has recently dug a passage!
Yes, yes, that's certainly right!
DE GIETER
28

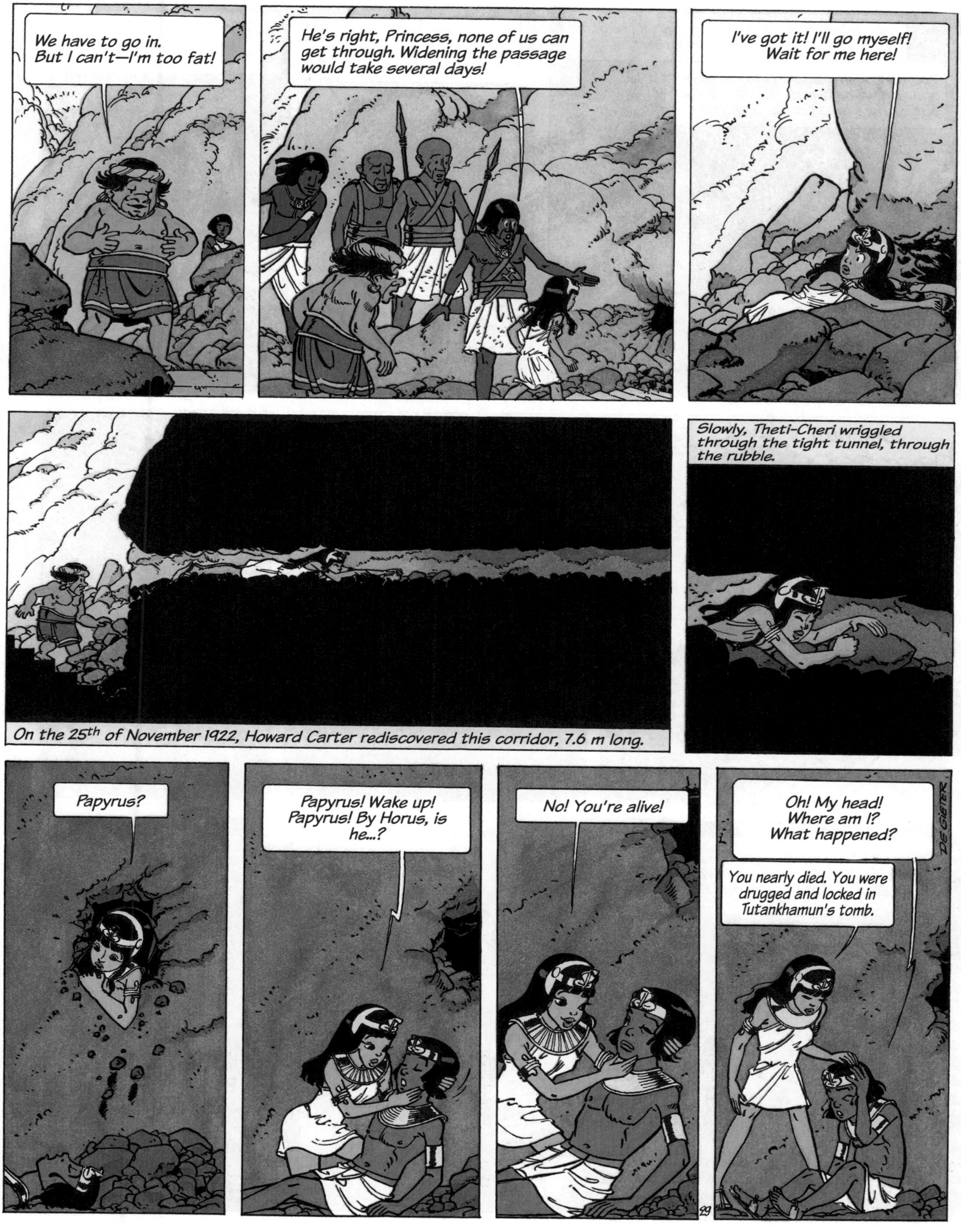

We have to go in. But I can't—I'm too fat!
He's right, Princess, none of us can get through. Widening the passage would take several days!
I've got it! I'll go myself! Wait for me here!
On the 25th of November 1922, Howard Carter rediscovered this corridor, 7.6 m long.
Slowly, Theti-Cheri wriggled through the tight tunnel, through the rubble.
Papyrus?
Papyrus! Wake up! Papyrus! By Horus, is he...?
No! You're alive!
Oh! My head! Where am I? What happened?
You nearly died. You were drugged and locked in Tutankhamun's tomb.
DE GIETER

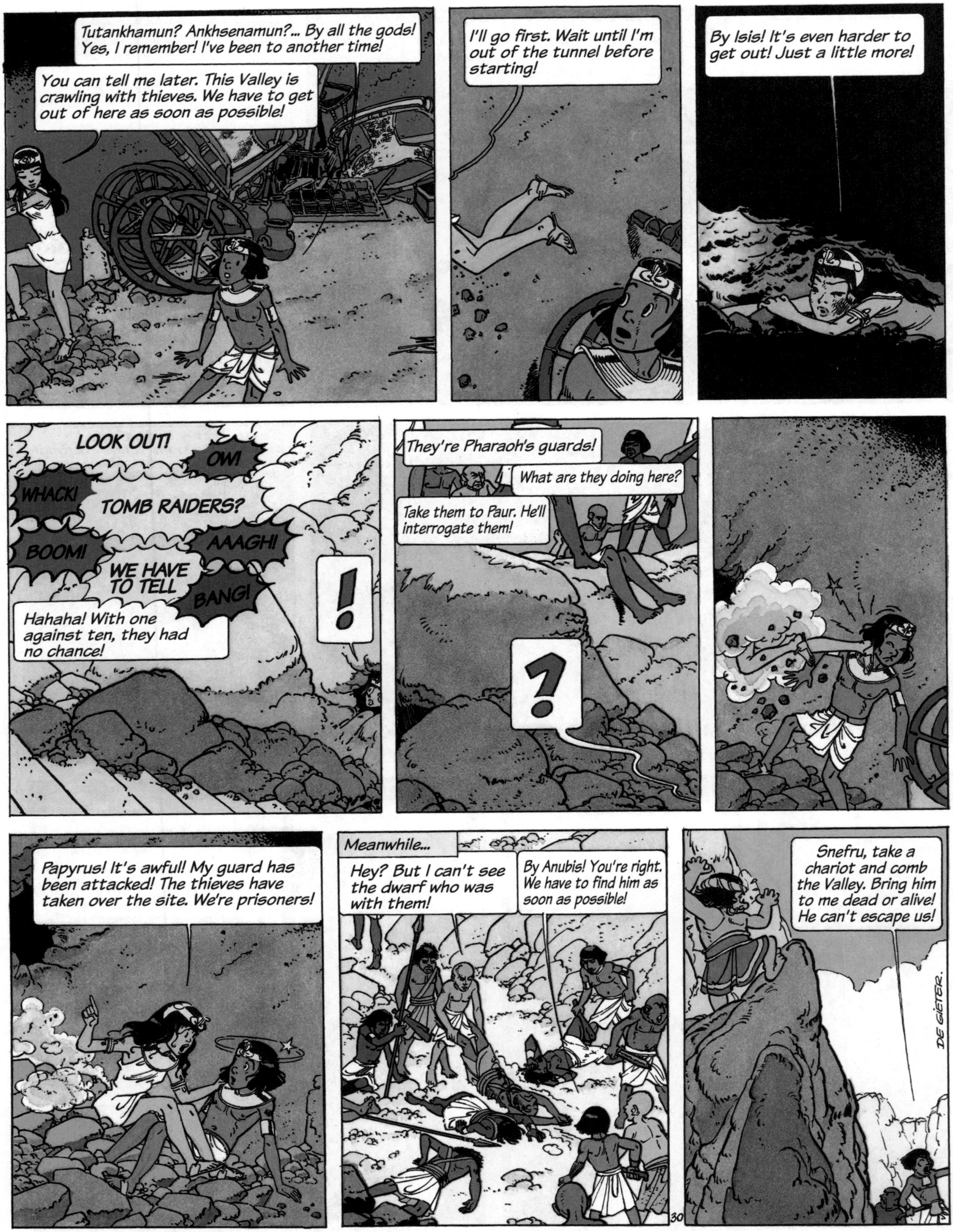

Tutankhamun? Ankhsenamun?... By all the gods! Yes, I remember! I've been to another time!
You can tell me later. This Valley is crawling with thieves. We have to get out of here as soon as possible!
I'll go first. Wait until I'm out of the tunnel before starting!
By Isis! It's even harder to get out! Just a little more!
LOOK OUT!
OW!
WHACK!
TOMB RAIDERS?
BOOM!
AAAGH!
WE HAVE TO TELL
BANG!
Hahaha! With one against ten, they had no chance!
!
They're Pharaoh's guards!
What are they doing here?
Take them to Paur. He'll interrogate them!
?
Papyrus! It's awful! My guard has been attacked! The thieves have taken over the site. We're prisoners!
Meanwhile...
Hey? But I can't see the dwarf who was with them!
By Anubis! You're right. We have to find him as soon as possible!
Snefru, take a chariot and comb the Valley. Bring him to me dead or alive! He can't escape us!
DE GIETER.
30

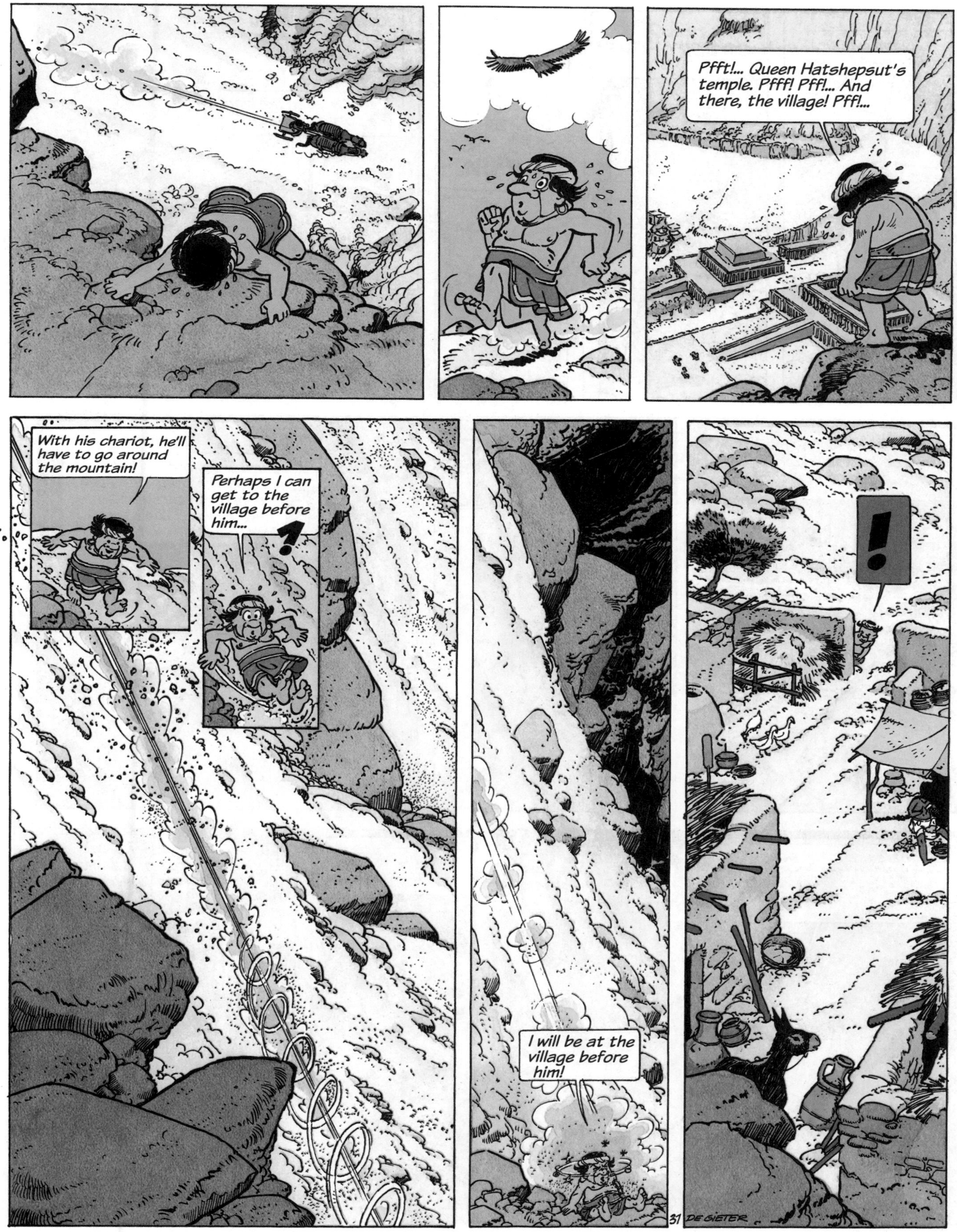
Pfft!... Queen Hatshepsut's temple. Pfff! Pff!... And there, the village! Pff!...
With his chariot, he'll have to go around the mountain!
Perhaps I can get to the village before him...
I will be at the village before him!
!
31 DE GIETER

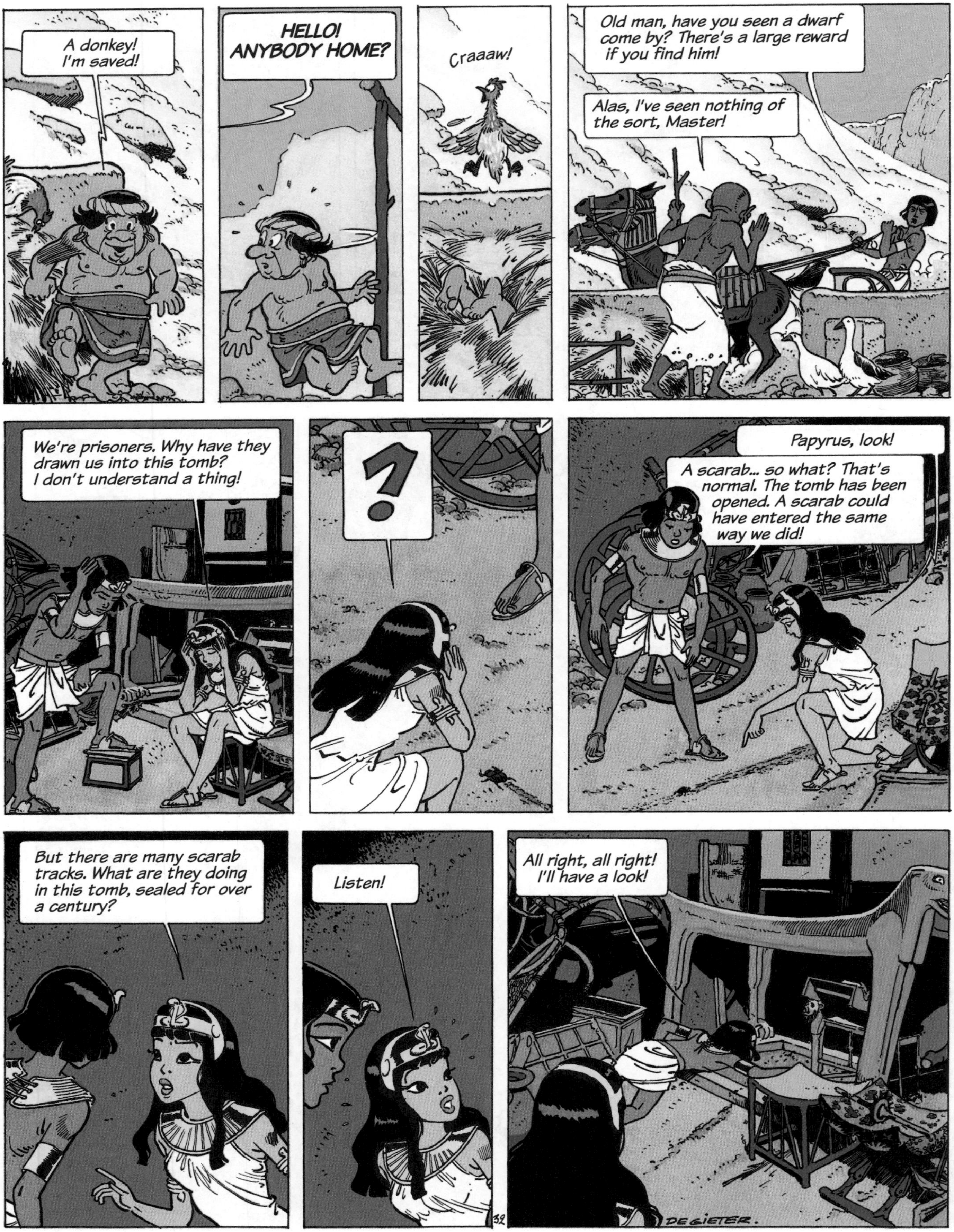

A donkey! I'm saved!
HELLO! ANYBODY HOME?
Craaaw!
Old man, have you seen a dwarf come by? There's a large reward if you find him!
Alas, I've seen nothing of the sort, Master!
We're prisoners. Why have they drawn us into this tomb? I don't understand a thing!
?
Papyrus, look!
A scarab... so what? That's normal. The tomb has been opened. A scarab could have entered the same way we did!
But there are many scarab tracks. What are they doing in this tomb, sealed for over a century?
Listen!
All right, all right! I'll have a look!
32
DE GIETER.

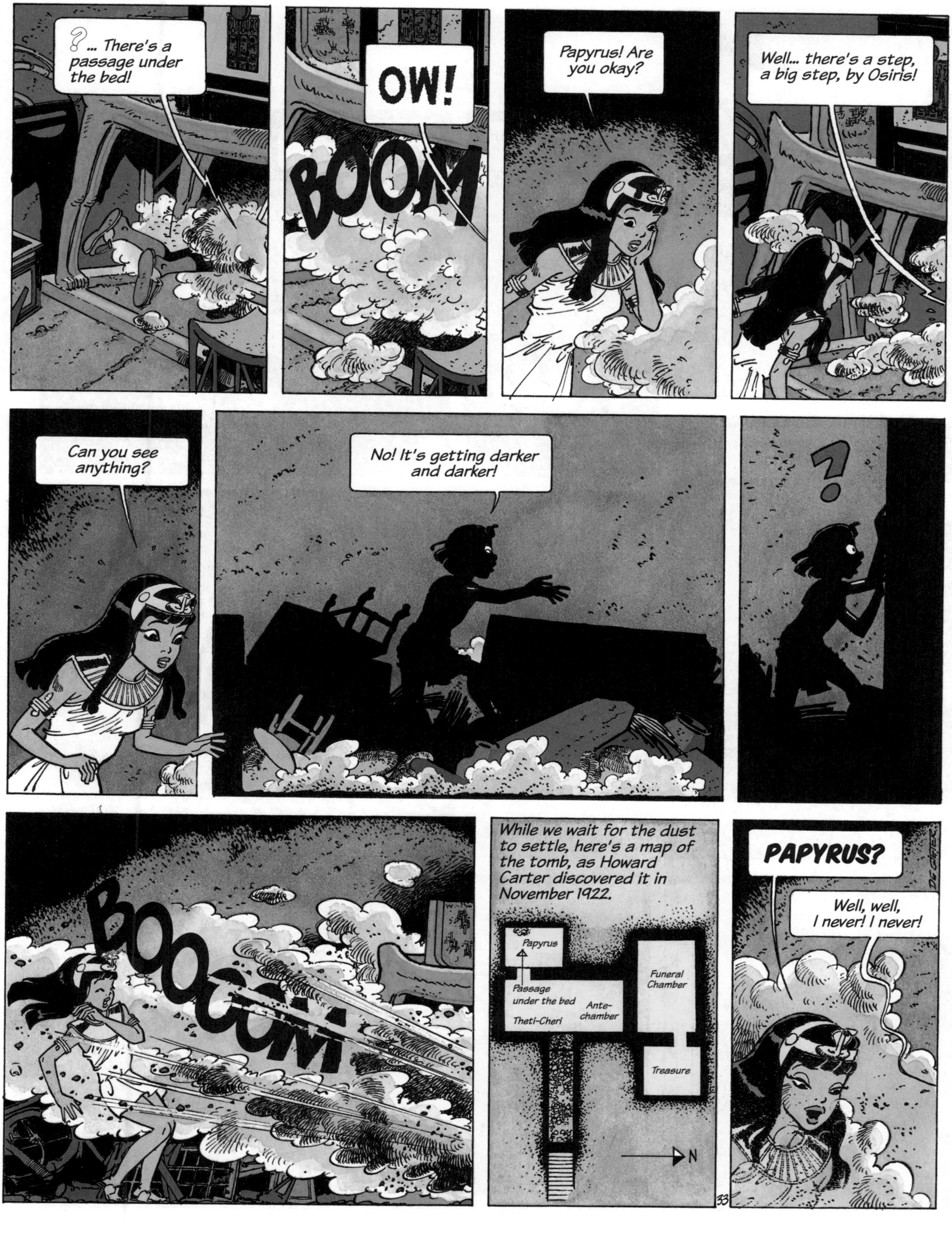
? ... There's a passage under the bed!
OW!
BOOM
Papyrus! Are you okay?
Well... there's a step, a big step, by Osiris!
Can you see anything?
No! It's getting darker and darker!
?
BOOOOOM
While we wait for the dust to settle, here's a map of the tomb, as Howard Carter discovered it in November 1922.
Papyrus
Passage under the bed
Theti-Cheri
Ante-chamber
Funeral Chamber
Treasure
N
PAPYRUS?
Well, well, I never! I never!
33

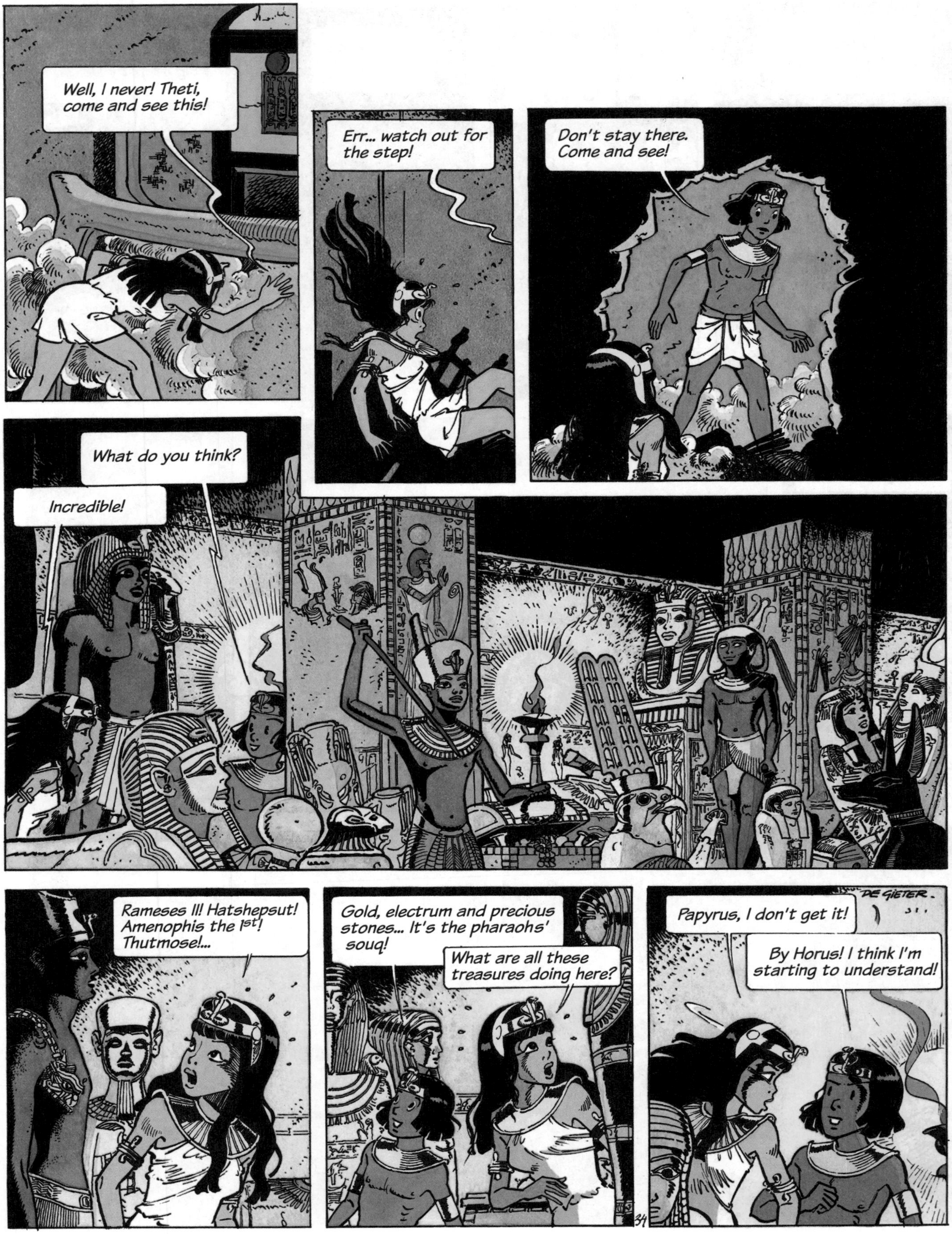
Well, I never! Theti, come and see this!
Err... watch out for the step!
Don't stay there. Come and see!
What do you think?
Incredible!
Rameses II! Hatshepsut! Amenophis the 1st! Thutmose!...
Gold, electrum and precious stones... It's the pharaohs' souq!
What are all these treasures doing here?
Papyrus, I don't get it!
By Horus! I think I'm starting to understand!
DE GIETER
34

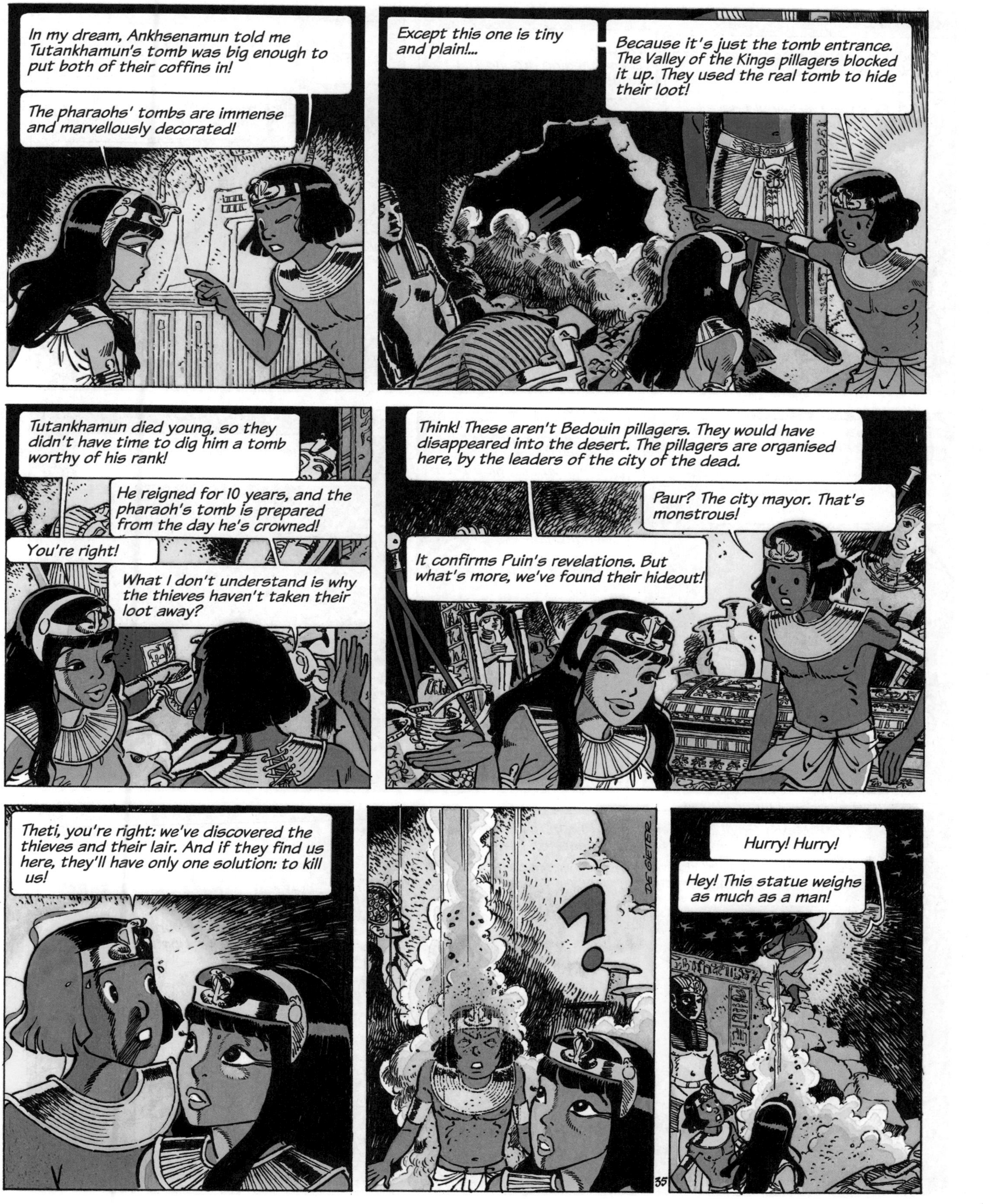
In my dream, Ankhsenamun told me Tutankhamun's tomb was big enough to put both of their coffins in!
The pharaohs' tombs are immense and marvellously decorated!
Except this one is tiny and plain!...
Because it's just the tomb entrance. The Valley of the Kings pillagers blocked it up. They used the real tomb to hide their loot!
Tutankhamun died young, so they didn't have time to dig him a tomb worthy of his rank!
He reigned for 10 years, and the pharaoh's tomb is prepared from the day he's crowned!
You're right!
What I don't understand is why the thieves haven't taken their loot away?
Think! These aren't Bedouin pillagers. They would have disappeared into the desert. The pillagers are organised here, by the leaders of the city of the dead.
Paur? The city mayor. That's monstrous!
It confirms Puin's revelations. But what's more, we've found their hideout!
Theti, you're right: we've discovered the thieves and their lair. And if they find us here, they'll have only one solution: to kill us!
?
DE GIETER
Hurry! Hurry!
Hey! This statue weighs as much as a man!
35

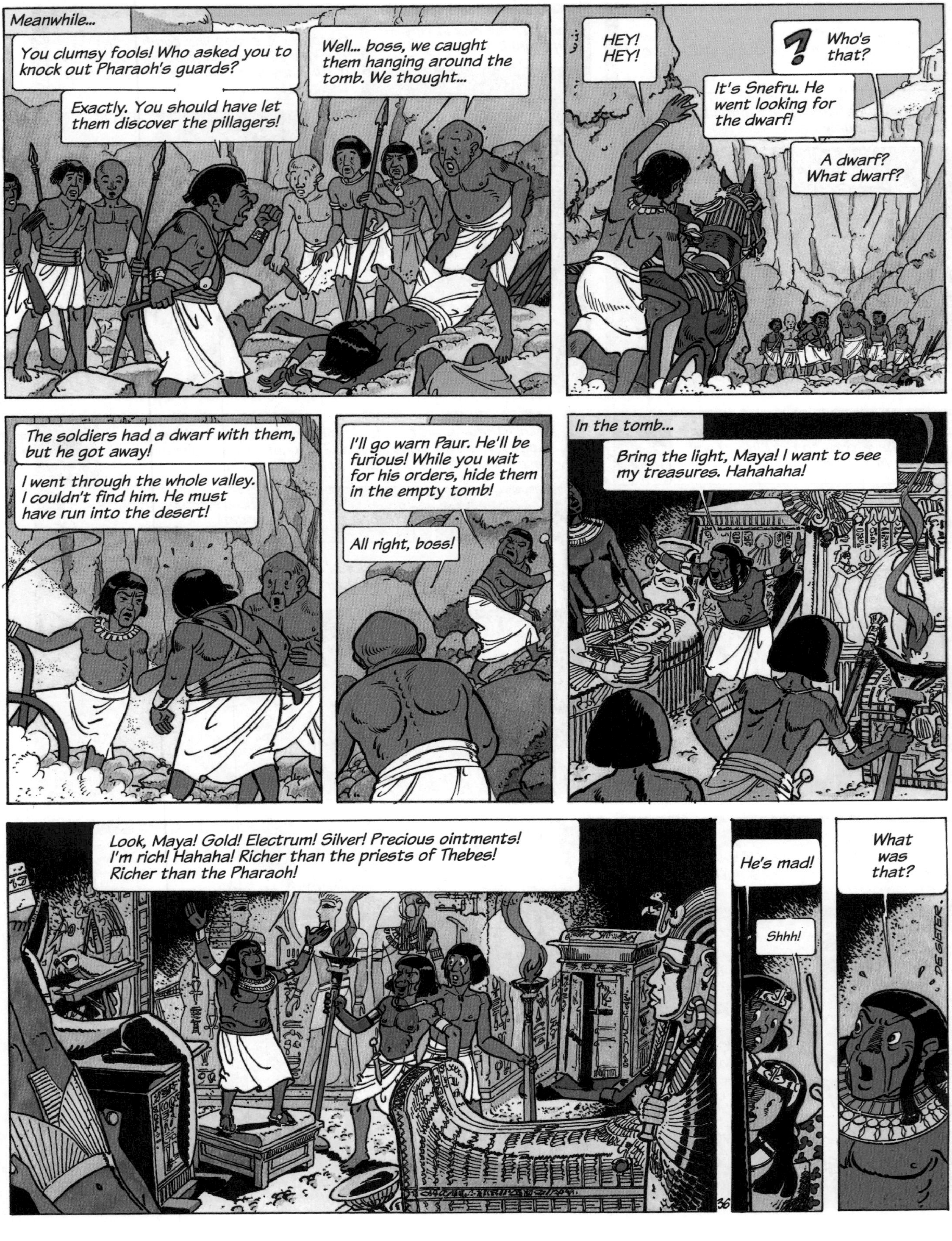
Meanwhile...
You clumsy fools! Who asked you to knock out Pharaoh's guards?
Exactly. You should have let them discover the pillagers!
Well... boss, we caught them hanging around the tomb. We thought...
HEY! HEY!
? Who's that?
It's Snefru. He went looking for the dwarf!
A dwarf? What dwarf?
The soldiers had a dwarf with them, but he got away!
I went through the whole valley. I couldn't find him. He must have run into the desert!
I'll go warn Paur. He'll be furious! While you wait for his orders, hide them in the empty tomb!
All right, boss!
In the tomb...
Bring the light, Maya! I want to see my treasures. Hahahaha!
Look, Maya! Gold! Electrum! Silver! Precious ointments! I'm rich! Hahaha! Richer than the priests of Thebes! Richer than the Pharaoh!
He's mad!
Shhh!
What was that?
DE GIETER
36

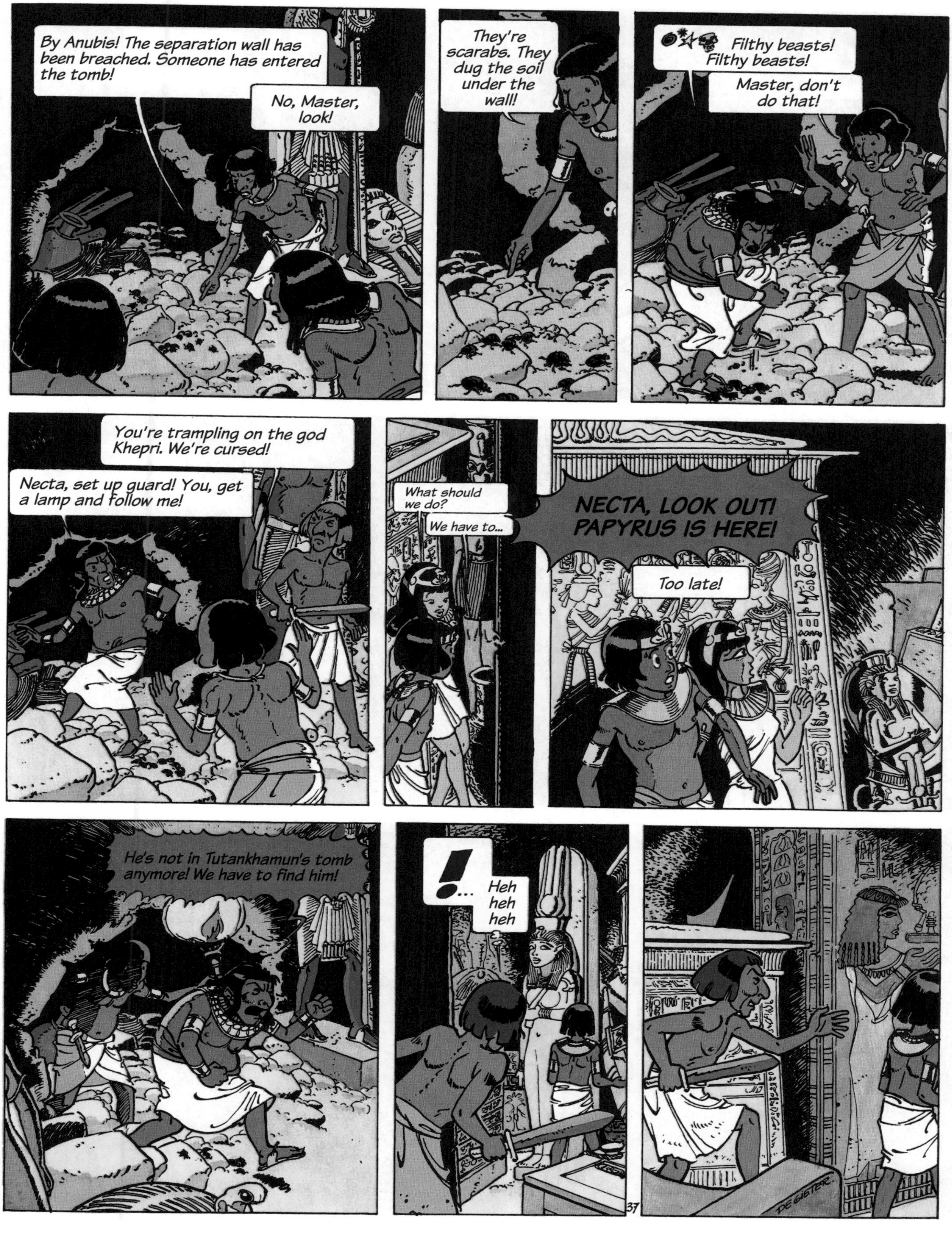
By Anubis! The separation wall has been breached. Someone has entered the tomb!
No, Master, look!
They're scarabs. They dug the soil under the wall!
Filthy beasts! Filthy beasts!
Master, don't do that!
You're trampling on the god Khepri. We're cursed!
Necta, set up guard! You, get a lamp and follow me!
What should we do?
We have to...
NECTA, LOOK OUT! PAPYRUS IS HERE!
Too late!
He's not in Tutankhamun's tomb anymore! We have to find him!
!...
Heh heh heh
DE GIETER
37

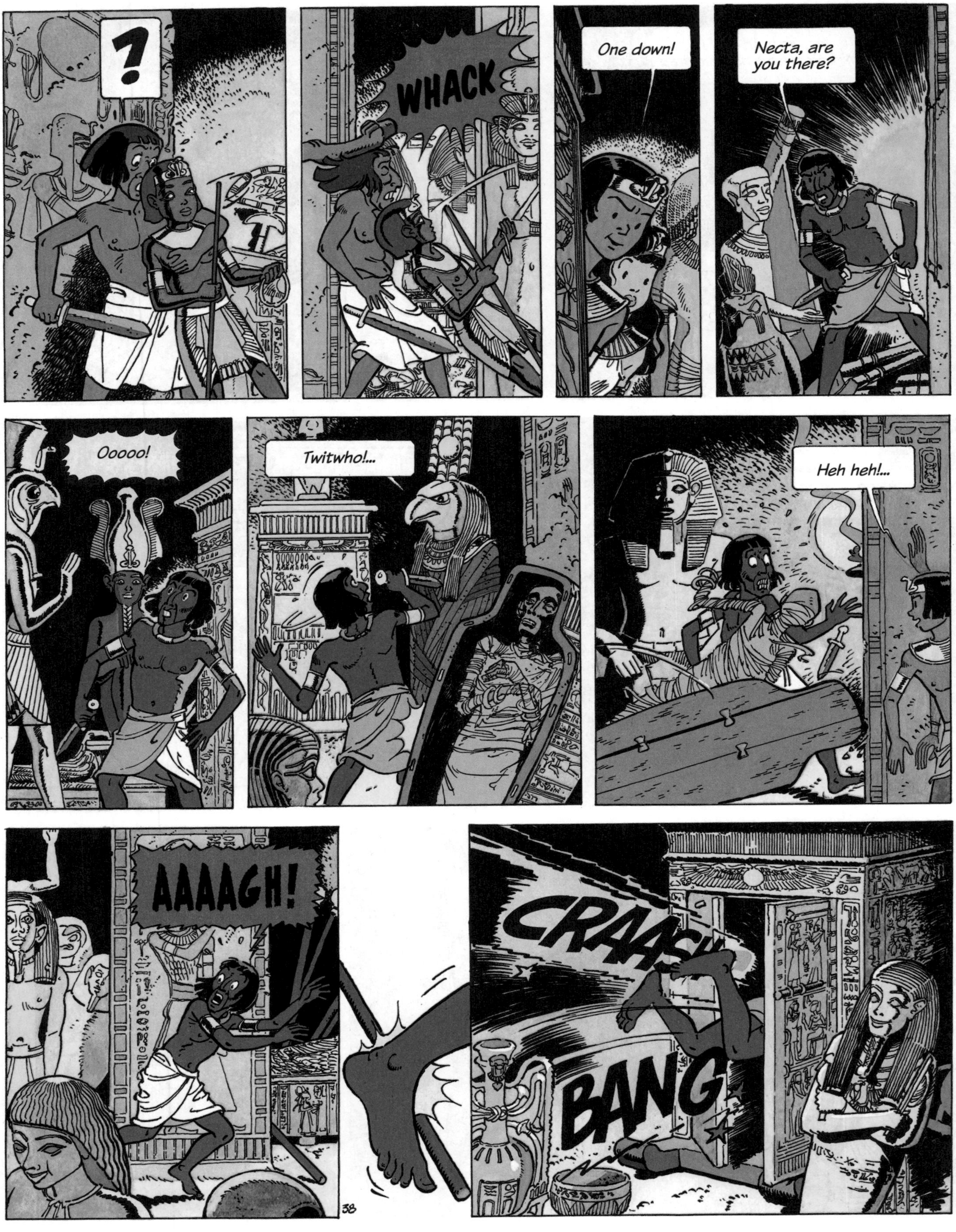
?
WHACK
One down!
Necta, are you there?
Ooooo!
Twitwho!...
Heh heh!...
AAAAGH!
CRAASH
BANG
38

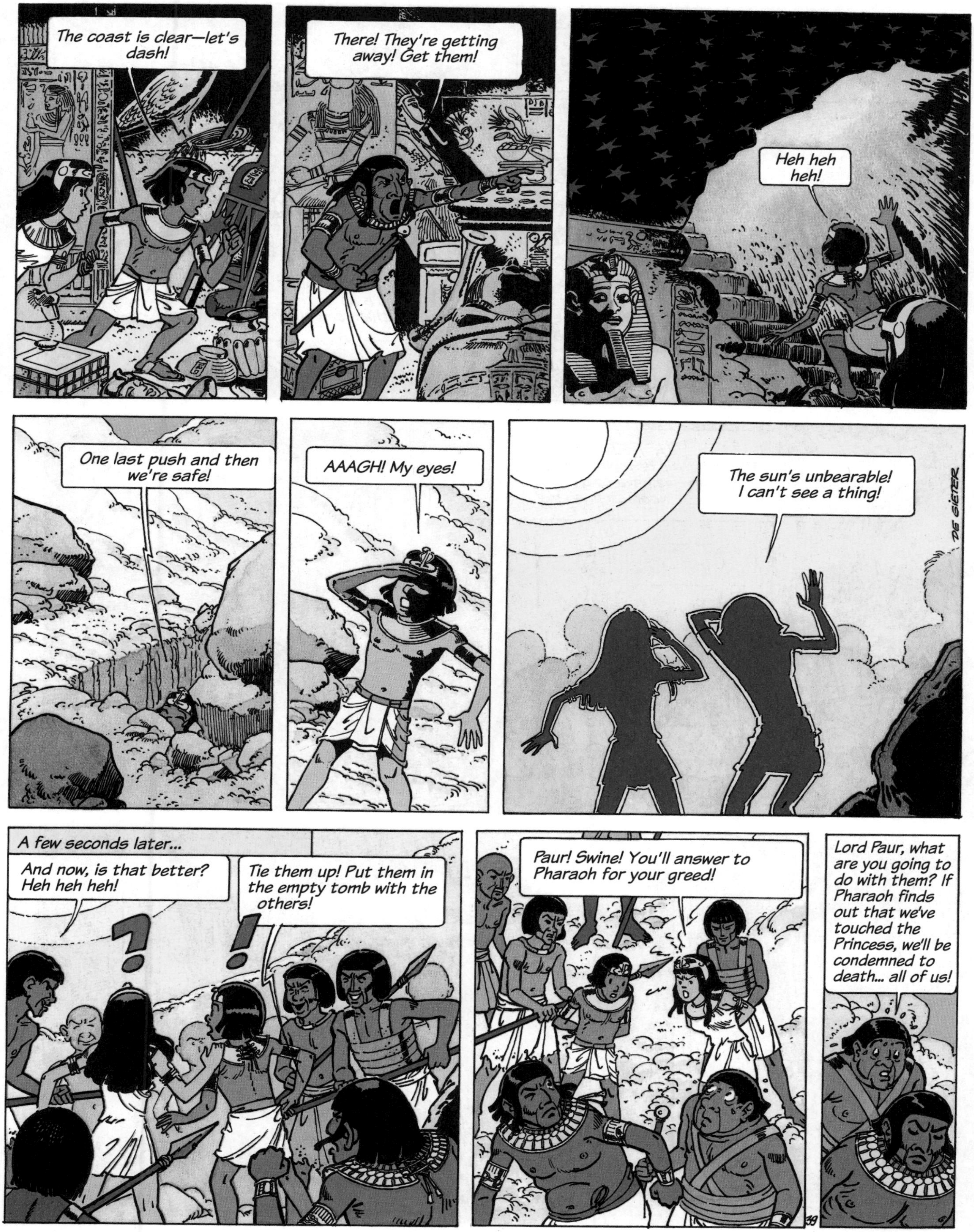
The coast is clear—let's dash!
There! They're getting away! Get them!
Heh heh heh!
One last push and then we're safe!
AAAGH! My eyes!
The sun's unbearable! I can't see a thing!
DE GIETER
A few seconds later...
And now, is that better? Heh heh heh!
?
!
Tie them up! Put them in the empty tomb with the others!
Paur! Swine! You'll answer to Pharaoh for your greed!
Lord Paur, what are you going to do with them? If Pharaoh finds out that we've touched the Princess, we'll be condemned to death... all of us!
39

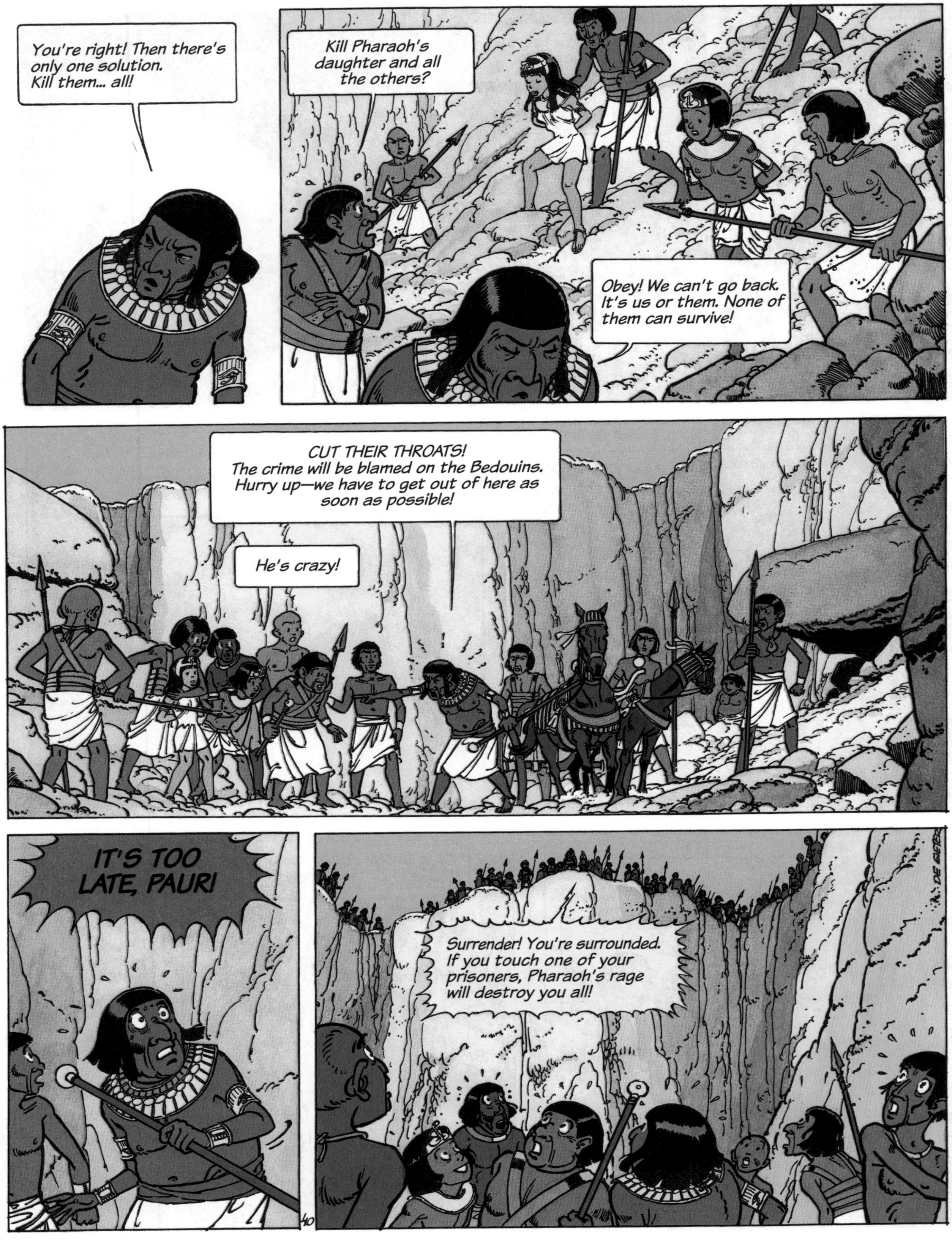
You're right! Then there's only one solution. Kill them... all!
Kill Pharaoh's daughter and all the others?
Obey! We can't go back. It's us or them. None of them can survive!
CUT THEIR THROATS! The crime will be blamed on the Bedouins. Hurry up—we have to get out of here as soon as possible!
He's crazy!
IT'S TOO LATE, PAUR!
Surrender! You're surrounded. If you touch one of your prisoners, Pharaoh's rage will destroy you all!
DE GIETER
40

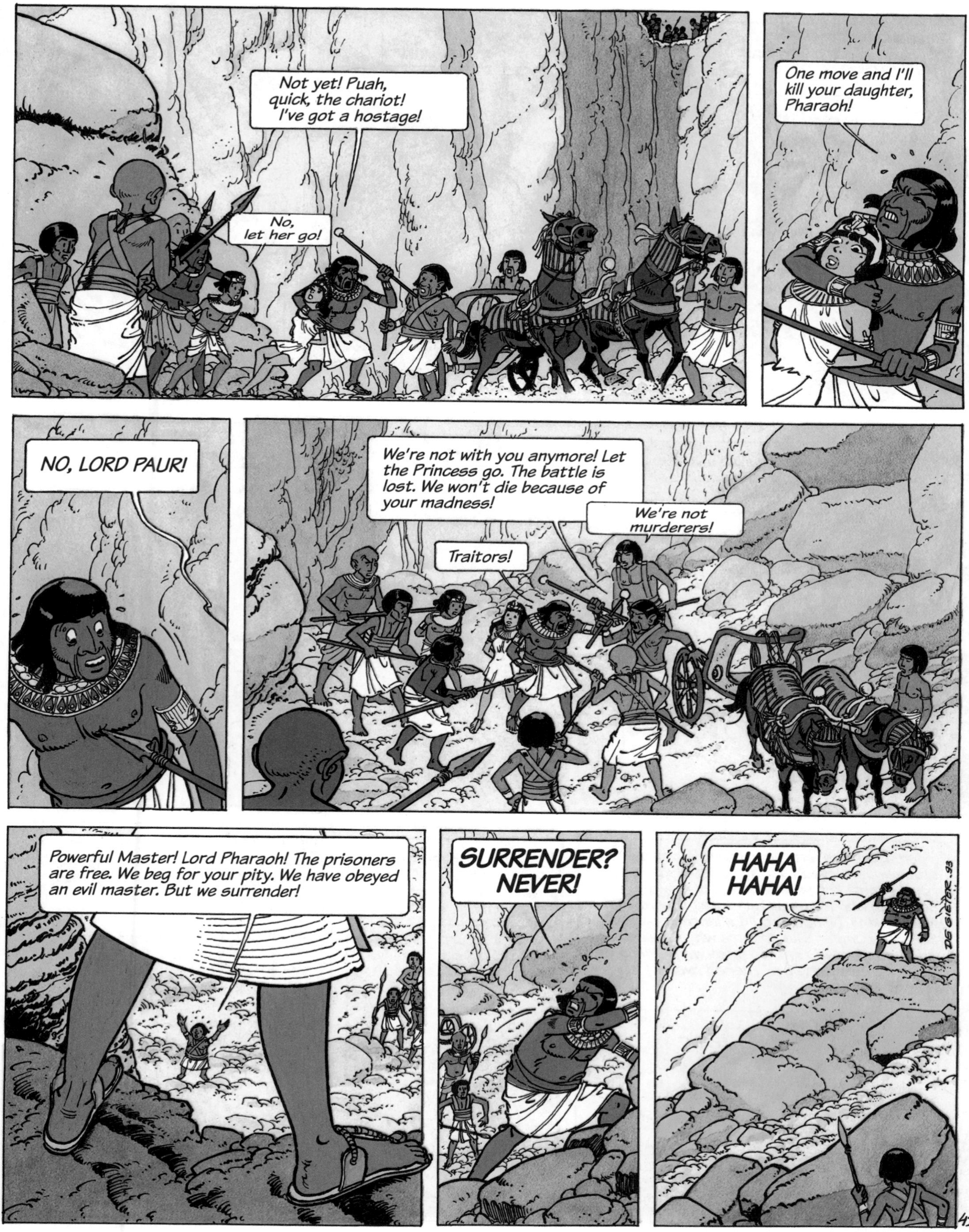
Not yet! Puah, quick, the chariot! I've got a hostage!
No, let her go!
One move and I'll kill your daughter, Pharaoh!
NO, LORD PAUR!
We're not with you anymore! Let the Princess go. The battle is lost. We won't die because of your madness!
We're not murderers!
Traitors!
Powerful Master! Lord Pharaoh! The prisoners are free. We beg for your pity. We have obeyed an evil master. But we surrender!
SURRENDER? NEVER!
HAHA HAHA!
DE GIETER 93
41

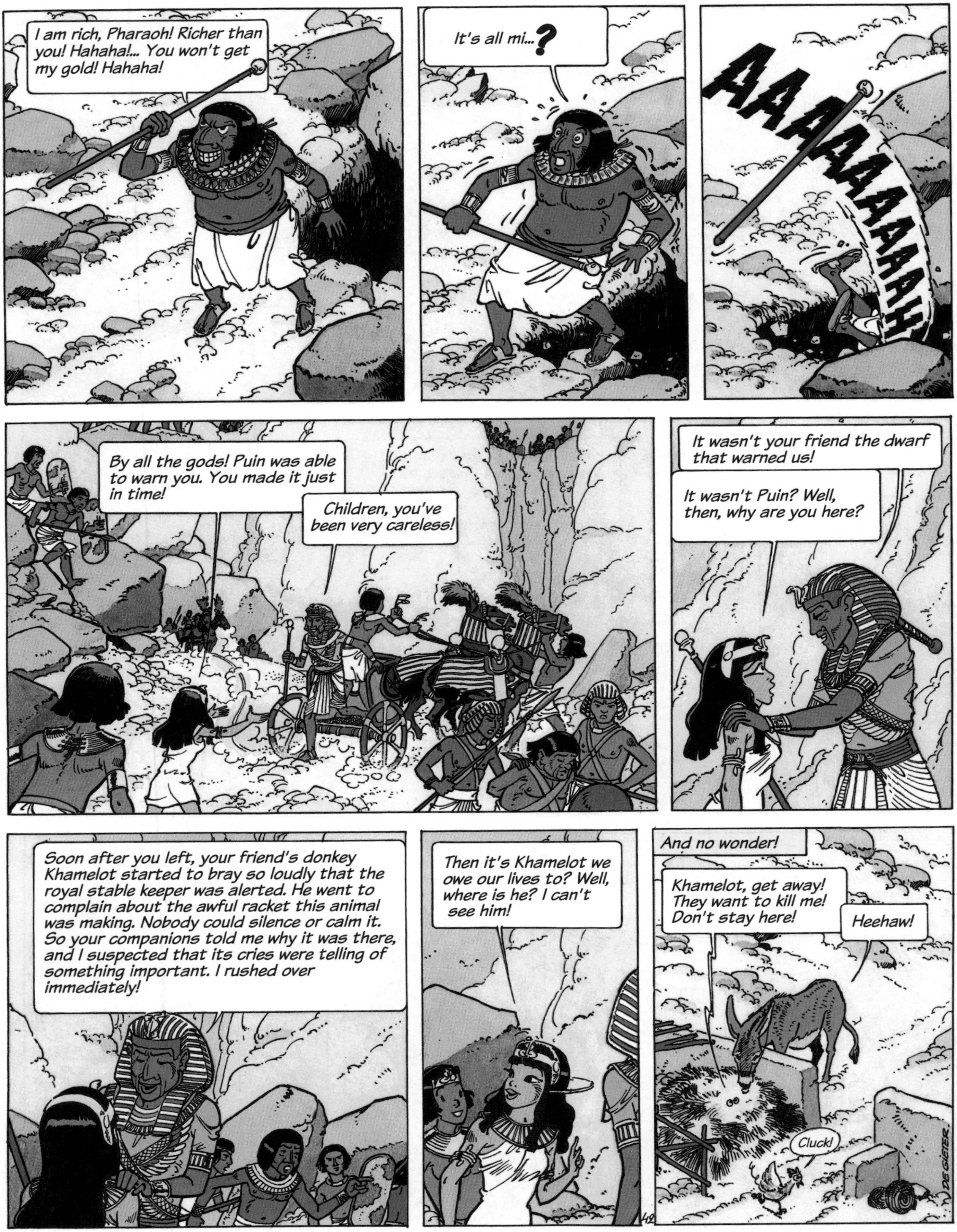
I am rich, Pharaoh! Richer than you! Hahaha!... You won't get my gold! Hahaha!
It's all mi...?
AAAAAAAAAAAAH
By all the gods! Puin was able to warn you. You made it just in time!
Children, you've been very careless!
It wasn't your friend the dwarf that warned us!
It wasn't Puin? Well, then, why are you here?
Soon after you left, your friend's donkey Khamelot started to bray so loudly that the royal stable keeper was alerted. He went to complain about the awful racket this animal was making. Nobody could silence or calm it. So your companions told me why it was there, and I suspected that its cries were telling of something important. I rushed over immediately!
Then it's Khamelot we owe our lives to? Well, where is he? I can't see him!
And no wonder!
Khamelot, get away! They want to kill me! Don't stay here!
Heehaw!
Cluck!
DE GIETER
42

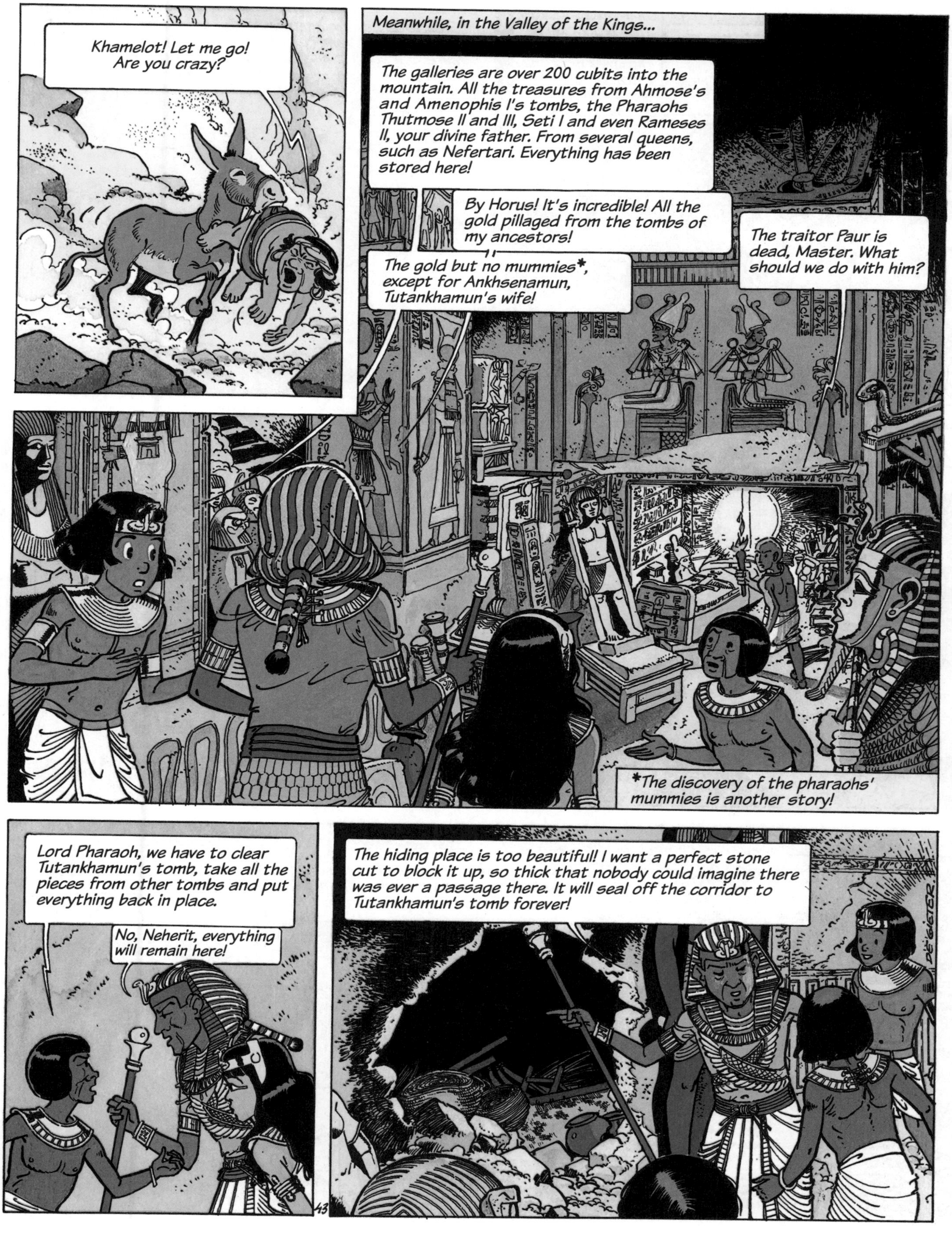

Khamelot! Let me go! Are you crazy?
Meanwhile, in the Valley of the Kings...
The galleries are over 200 cubits into the mountain. All the treasures from Ahmose's and Amenophis I's tombs, the Pharaohs Thutmose II and III, Seti I and even Rameses II, your divine father. From several queens, such as Nefertari. Everything has been stored here!
By Horus! It's incredible! All the gold pillaged from the tombs of my ancestors!
The gold but no mummies*, except for Ankhsenamun, Tutankhamun's wife!
The traitor Paur is dead, Master. What should we do with him?
*The discovery of the pharaohs' mummies is another story!
Lord Pharaoh, we have to clear Tutankhamun's tomb, take all the pieces from other tombs and put everything back in place.
No, Neherit, everything will remain here!
The hiding place is too beautiful! I want a perfect stone cut to block it up, so thick that nobody could imagine there was ever a passage there. It will seal off the corridor to Tutankhamun's tomb forever!
DE GIETER
43

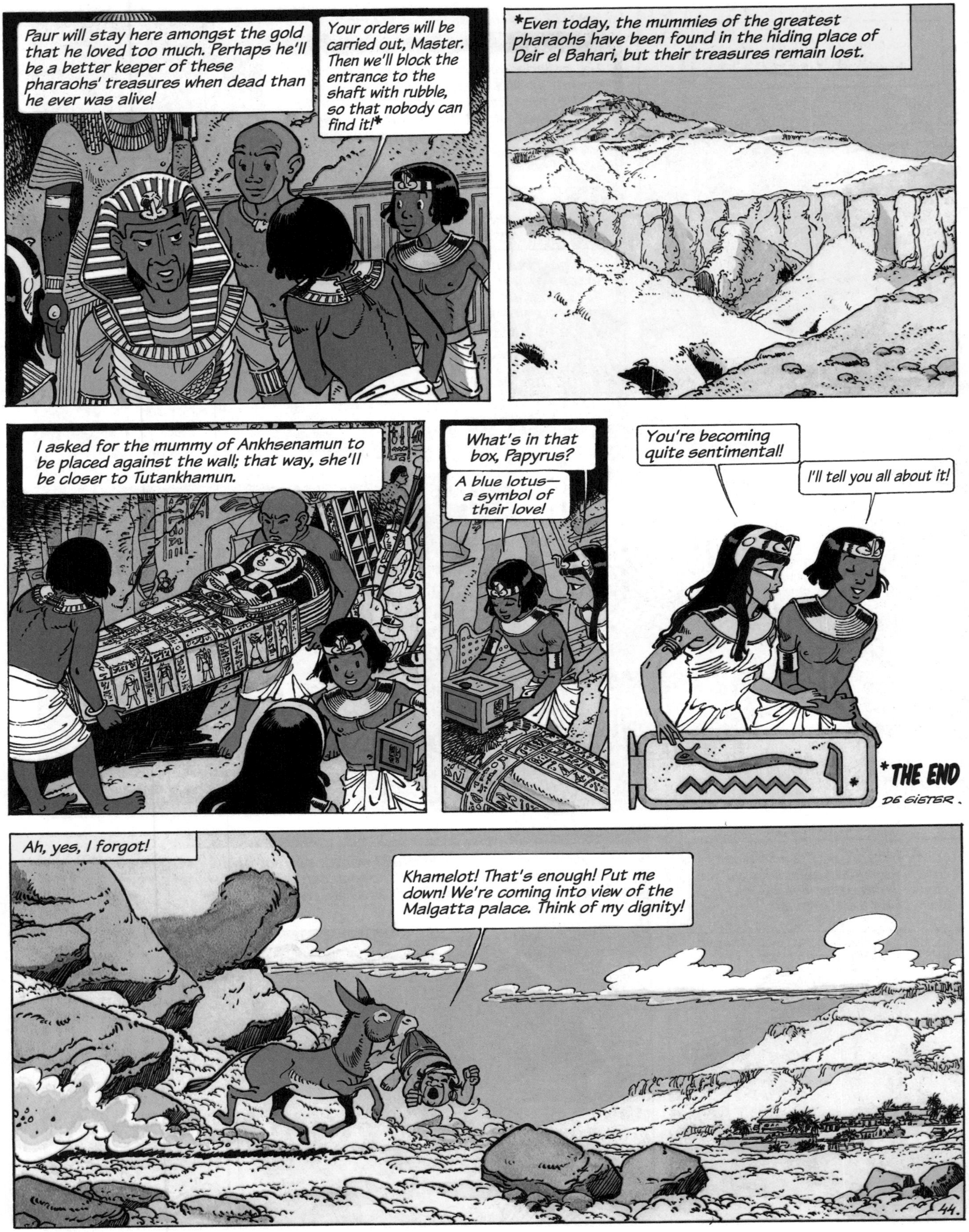
Paur will stay here amongst the gold that he loved too much. Perhaps he'll be a better keeper of these pharaohs' treasures when dead than he ever was alive!
Your orders will be carried out, Master. Then we'll block the entrance to the shaft with rubble, so that nobody can find it!*
*Even today, the mummies of the greatest pharaohs have been found in the hiding place of Deir el Bahari, but their treasures remain lost.
I asked for the mummy of Ankhsenamun to be placed against the wall; that way, she'll be closer to Tutankhamun.
What's in that box, Papyrus?
A blue lotus— a symbol of their love!
You're becoming quite sentimental!
I'll tell you all about it!
*THE END
DE GIETER.
Ah, yes, I forgot!
Khamelot! That's enough! Put me down! We're coming into view of the Malgatta palace. Think of my dignity!
44.

1 - THE RAMESES' REVENGE

2 - IMHOTEP'S TRANSFORMATION

COMING SOON

3 - TUTANKHAMUN
THE ASSASSINATED PHARAOH

4 - THE EVIL MUMMIES

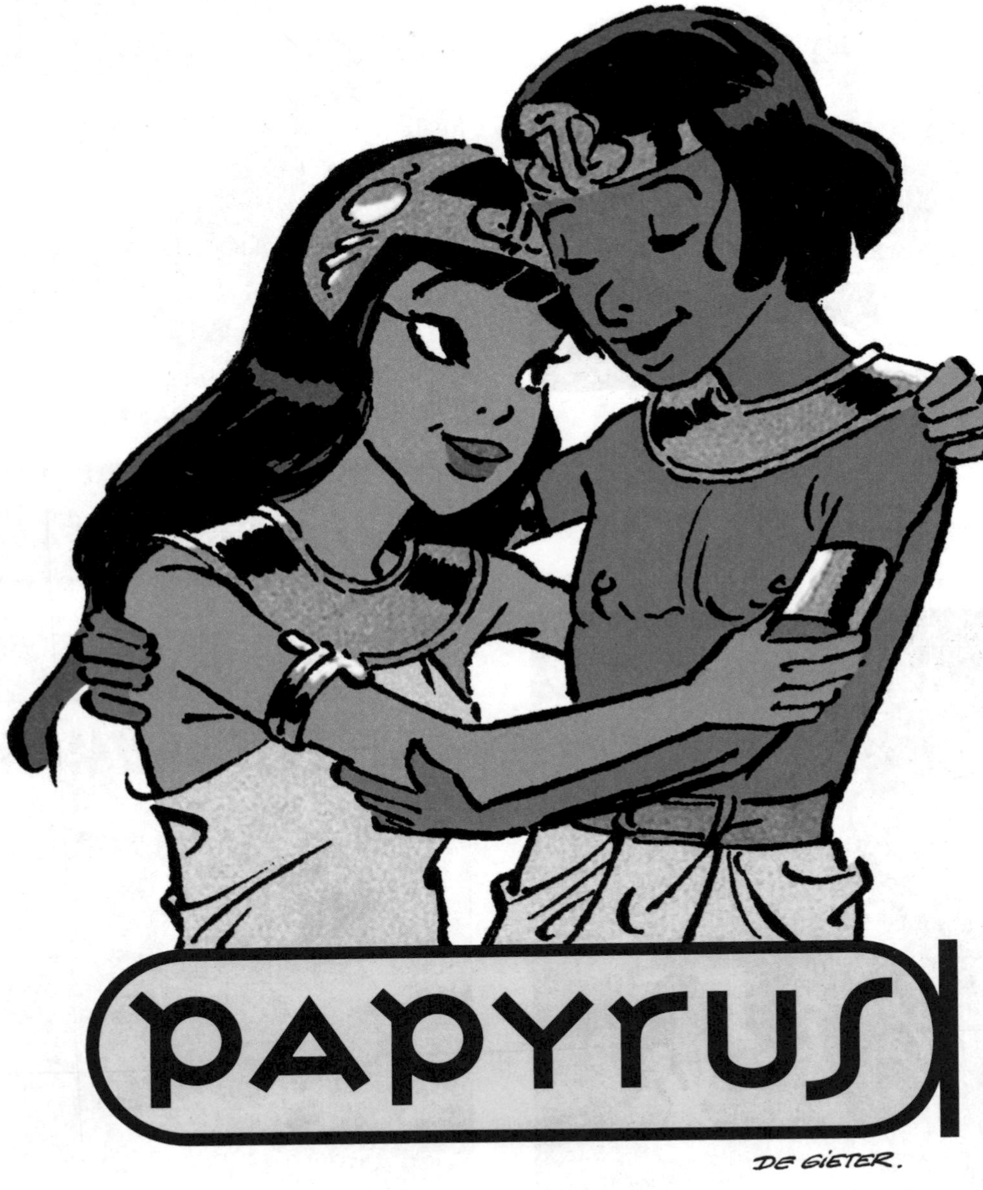
papyrus
DE GIETER.